W9-ARE-996

Treating Children in Groups

A Behavioral Approach

SHELDON D. ROSE

TREATING CHILDREN IN GROUPS

Jossey-Bass Inc., Publishers
San Francisco · Washington · London · 1972

TREATING CHILDREN IN GROUPS
A Behavioral Approach
by Sheldon D. Rose

Published in Great Britain by
Jossey-Bass, Inc., Publishers
St. George's House
44 Hatton Garden, London E.C.1

Library of Congress Catalogue Card Number LC 78-189609

International Standard Book Number ISBN 0-87589-131-4

Manufactured in the United States of America

JACKET DESIGN BY WILLI BAUM

FIRST EDITION

Code 7214

The Jossey-Bass
Behavioral Science Series

Preface

Treating Children in Groups focuses on behavioral change in therapy; behavior not personality is the target of change. If treatment is successful the client should be able to cope more adequately with and to live more happily in the world about him. Because behavior is accessible, it lends itself to being evaluated at any point in treatment. If, then, treatment is successful, the client, the people who surround him, and the therapist have clear indications of this success. But *Treating Children in Groups* is about a particular kind of behavioral therapy—one which occurs in small, face-to-face groups. The group provides an unusual set of means as well as a context for treatment. The behaviors on which the treatment focuses are usually though not exclusively those which are readily practiced in groups, such as skills in making and keeping friends and new ways of responding to others. Although the general principles described here are relevant to all age groups, the specific applications, the particular models, and the examples pertain primarily to boys and girls. The emphasis is on children ranging from eight to twelve years of age, but examples cover children as young as four and as old as seventeen.

Treating Children in Groups attempts to teach the reader to apply the principles of behavior modification to patients, clients, or students. Although many books have been written about this subject, this is one of the first to demonstrate how many of these principles can be applied to the small-group treatment of children. Thus, I describe and illustrate the basic concepts of a behavioral approach with examples derived chiefly from group situations. I also clarify such group level concepts as group goals, group composition, group treatment plans, attraction to the group, and group structures in behavioral terms.

Among the many procedures discussed as they apply to the group situation are individual and group contingencies, behavioral contracting, modeling, behavioral rehearsal, and individual and group desensitization. I show how these procedures can be used to attain behaviorally defined treatment goals. And I demonstrate how these procedures can be used to alter the attraction to the group and such group structures as norms, leadership and status arrangements, and patterns of communication.

I describe several groups in which the behavioral approach can be applied. The first comprises children similar in age and development but with diverse presenting problems. A second group consists of only one or two target clients and two or more model children included for the purpose of imitation of their behavior. The third is a transition group in which institutionalized children are taught those behaviors they need to negotiate their return to community, foster home, home, or school. The fourth model is a cross-age tutor-training group in which the clients learn behaviors they need to tutor younger children.

Treating Children in Groups is designed for training or retraining the group therapist, whether he is a school social worker, a school counselor, a school psychologist, a juvenile probation officer, a street worker, a club leader, a special education teacher, a psychiatrist, a psychiatric social worker, or a group aide. The book is written as a manual which stresses how to apply the many principles illustrated. Only a sample of the literature supporting the approach and its specific principles is presented.

For the reader well schooled in learning theory and behavior modification, much of the material presented here is not new. If he is concerned with applications to group settings, he should find the examples and chapters devoted to modifying group attractiveness and structure most useful. For the reader schooled in group dynamics but uninformed about behavior modification, a supplementary text in behavior modification (for example, Bandura, 1969) should be helpful in acquiring sufficient knowledge on the subject. For the novice in group treatment with limited knowledge about behavior modification, broad supplementary training may be necessary before he can apply the lessons of this book. For the curious nontherapist who wishes simply to compare this approach with others or to explore an area of interest, *Treating Children in Books* should be an interesting introduction.

The theoretical sources of this book are several. Its behavior modification theory draws heavily upon the work of Skinner (1953) and his followers, of Bandura (1969), and of Wolpe (1969). It is based also upon the group concepts presented most succinctly by Cartwright and Zander (1968) and their colleagues. And since it is about a goal-oriented approach to group treatment, it draws upon the ideas of Vinter (1967) and his associates. Because of the use of these diverse sources, the reader may have difficulty in discovering a unified theoretical basis. However, the clinician cannot wait for the development of such a theory.

Like most books *Group Treatment of Children* is the result of many different contributions by many people. I am grateful to my students, from whose experience many of the examples are derived. I must confess to a very special appreciation for the work of one former student who as a school social worker has tried out and helped develop many of the ideas presented here—my wife, Cynthia. I am also indebted to my colleagues and former students at the Neighborhood Service Organization (Detroit), who shared as staff of the Hartwig Project in early attempts at behavioral group treatment with children. I wish to express my appreciation to Robert Vinter and his colleagues at the University of Michigan, who introduced me to goal-oriented group treatment, and to Edwin

Thomas, who introduced me to behavior modification. I am grateful for the comments and patience of my present colleagues at the University of Wisconsin, who have had to endure my preoccupation with the subject of this book. I also express my appreciation to the secretarial staff of the School of Social Work of the University of Wisconsin, who assisted in the typing of the several drafts of this book and who improved my spelling and syntax immeasurably. And finally I am especially indebted to Ruth Schmidt, whose editorial assistance came at a time when I was rapidly growing weary of further work on the book. Without the assistance of these and many others who have not been mentioned, *Treating Children in Groups* would never have been written. Yet, for the final form and content, I alone remain responsible.

Madison SHELDON D. ROSE
February 1972

Contents

Treating Children in Groups

A Behavioral Approach

I

Modifying Behavior in Groups

Walter: *I guess I'm awfully nervous. Dad says I cry too much.*
Larry: *I get in lots of fights, so they kicked me out of school.*
Greg: *Just cause I won't do no chores, my ma always yells at me.*
Bruce: *I don't like rough kids, I don't like to get dirty or get picked on.*
Alan: *I don't like nothing at all, not you guys, not baseball, not anything.*
Martin: *No matter what they do, they can't make me go to school. Everybody makes fun of me.*

These six boys, ages ten and eleven, are learning to work and play together in a group and to live happily with others. Their teachers, parents, and other children in their immediate world have described them as nuisances and as failures; each has experienced rejection and long periods of unhappiness. The purpose of their group is to help them find new behaviors for dealing with their world—behaviors which no longer incur the wrath or ridicule of those around them. The group is both a set of means and the major context of treatment. A therapist, at least initially, serves as the guide; behavior and group modification are his major tools.

These boys are receiving group treatment. If one watches through a one-way mirror, he observes the therapist responding to desirable behavior (such as one child's offering another a toy) by issuing poker chips or tokens to the giver (reinforcement). The therapist tends to ignore undesirable behaviors (extinction) such as whining or pushing which do not disrupt the group. Should a child get completely out of control, the therapist separates him from the others until he has calmed down (time out from reinforcement), then asks him to return to the group and continue as before. There are many group tasks of short duration during the ninety minute meeting. Some are school simulated activities, others are physical games, and still others are arts and crafts projects. During most of these activities tokens are awarded for specific achievements. At the end of the meeting, each child takes the tokens he has earned and cashes them in for food, small toys, pencils, books, and other items in a "store" in the corner of the room.

Toward the end of the meeting the boys are observed sitting in a circle and discussing what each will work on during the week. One child says he will do at least one chore every day. He signs an agreement (contract) to that effect. Another agrees that he will increase his homework time to thirty minutes a day; another writes in his contract that he will play with his schoolmates a game he learned in the group meeting. A fourth boy is being helped by the others to determine what he could do to make more friends. Each boy eventually receives a behavioral assignment which can be performed before the next meeting and which can be observerd by a parent, teacher, or other person involved in his daily activities. In general, the boys seem to enjoy themselves, as evidenced by their early arrival, their tendency to linger at the end of the meeting, and their enthusiasm throughout the various activities. The passing observer, in fact, might have difficulty understanding why such boys have been referred for treatment.

The treatment described above involves more, of course, than the issuance of rewards or tokens at the right moment. Prior to the application of such change procedures, a determination is made of the client's specific problematic behaviors, and a method is devised for counting and charting these behaviors. The treatment recommends contracts between the child and the group regarding behaviors to be changed and the responsibility of each participant. Treatment procedures also include various forms of limits, program activities, models and rehearsal, cues, and desensitization procedures. When tokens or other rewards are used, treatment requires their gradual withdrawal (fading) and the gradual simulation in treatment conditions of the child's real world. This approach also involves the development of assignments which the child does at home, at school, and on the playground to carry out what he has learned in this laboratorylike treatment setting. And finally it includes special procedures to stabilize and transfer learning to other situations. It is a complex process, but the skills are learnable, by both the therapist and the child, and in a period of three to six months one can usually observe substantially changed patterns of behavior in the child.

Most of the principles expressed or implied in the above example are applicable to adults (Lazarus, 1965) as well as to children. However, the specific procedures and examples found in this book are derived primarily from research and experience with groups of children. The use of peer-group treatment of children in child guidance clinics, juvenile corrections institutions and homes, mental health clinics, and similar agencies has been rapidly expanding, and with this growth the need for a manual for group therapists has increased.

This book provides the group therapist with a set of explicit procedures for group treatment of children. I present a paradigm for determination of the problem; procedures to modify the child's behavior, cognitions, and attitudes; and techniques to modify group attributes such as cohesiveness, communication, norms, and subgroup structure. I draw upon three major sources for my treatment and concept model: behavior modification as represented by such authors as Skinner (1953), Ullmann and Krasner (1965), Bandura (1969), and Wolpe (1969); small group theory as explicated by Cartwright and Zander (1968); and the goal-oriented practice theory of group treatment suggested by Vinter (1967).

Ways and Means

To illustrate the techniques of behavior modification clearly, let us look at one group member and the treatment of her problem behavior. Sally was referred to the group because she was shy; that is, she did not play with other children, and, given a choice, she remained with adults. An observer at the first meeting counted fewer than five minutes per hour of playing time with other children. At the second meeting, the therapist smiled and praised Sally whenever she approached other children; when she approached the therapist or the observer, neither responded. At the end of this session she was playing with other children at the rate of twenty-five minutes per hour. At the end of a third session, in which Sally was praised only when playing with other children, she was spending forty minutes per hour with the others; this amount was almost the same as the average for all children in the group. By the sixth session praise and smiling were given at random, but the behavior remained (thirty-five to forty-five minutes per hour with other children). Since shyness is too general to be dealt with by using behavior modification, the therapist focused on altering Sally's pattern of choosing adult over peer group contact. The procedure used to alter this pattern provided the adult attention which Sally valued highly. In Sally's case, adult attention can be regarded as reinforcement because when it followed a given behavior, the frequency of that behavior increased. Conversely, when reinforcement was withheld, the accompanying behavior decreased. This process is called extinction. In order to establish procedure effectiveness, the behavior of the child was counted (monitored) before, during, and following the use of reinforcement and extinction.

The therapist in this example is using behavior modification—that is, any approach which applies the results of learning theory and experimental psychology to the problems of altering behavior (Ullmann and Krasner, 1965, p. 2). In this case one behavior (playing with children) was increased in frequency, and another (remaining with adults) was decreased. It would have also been within the scope of behavior modification to develop a new behavior, to eliminate a behavior, or to maintain a given frequency of a behavior. All learning theories postulate that behavior is controlled in certain ways by its environment. In the example above, the frequency of Sally's behaviors was modified by altering the events following them. (It would not be sufficient merely to alter Sally's behavior within the context of treatment only. Through adjustment of the ratio or frequency with which reinforcement is given, through variation of the conditions of treatment, and through application of other procedures, Sally can begin to carry over her learning in treatment to nontreatment situations. See Chapter Fourteen for a discussion of these principles.) This particular learning approach is called operant conditioning. An operant can be defined as a behavior that "operates" on the environment and produces some change in it (Tharp and Wetzel, 1969). In addition to reinforcement and extinction, aversive stimuli (punishment) following a given behavior also have implications for its frequency. The major foundation of behavior modification is that body of principles pertaining to the procedures by which reinforcement, extinction, punishment, and other techniques are administered. (These principles will be discussed in detail in Chapter Two.)

Another means by which learning can occur (behavior can be modified) is the observation of others' behavior. According to Bandura (1969), provided certain other prerequisites are met, one can develop intricate behavior patterns merely by observing models who are reinforced for their behavior. Since the group affords a wide range of models for each member, the use of modeling and related procedures is especially well suited to group treatment. In the following example we see how Tommy learned a new behavior by watching another group member.

Tommy was constantly teased by members of his class. Though large for his age, he responded only by crying or running away while his peers laughed. He wanted to learn how to tease back or even to ignore the behavior of the other children but he was afraid. In the group Tommy observed how Frank, a smaller boy, ignored teasing by the other group members. Frank just laughed and recited "sticks and stones. . . ." In this example, the therapist set up the group to tease Frank. He instructed Tommy to watch very carefully and rewarded him for his observation. After a while, Tommy began hesitatingly to try out some of the responses he observed. Although it took some time and coaching, one day, much to the surprise of the group members, when Tommy was teased, he too laughed and shouted "sticks and stones. . . ." As can be seen in this example, modeling and operant procedures are not independent, but are sufficiently distinct to warrant a description of their particular technology. (See Chapter Nine.)

Although most of the procedures in the behavioral approach to group treatment outlined here are derived from principles of operant conditioning and modeling, several procedures which are derived from classical or respondent conditioning might be applied in a case like the following. Every time Peter sees a dog he becomes anxious (his palms sweat, hands tremble, heart palpitates, breathing becomes labored), and he usually cries and runs away. The dog is a stimulus which elicits the respondent (autonomic) behaviors—in this case, anxiety. One of the several procedures for dealing with this problem is desensitization, which may be regarded as a form of respondent conditioning. In desensitization Peter is first taught to relax. After determining the variables which seem to contribute to Peter's anxiety—such as the kind of dog, the distance between him and the dog, the kind of noise the dog is making, and the dog's postures—a list of situations is written up and ranked from least to most anxiety producing. At one extreme is a picture of a sleeping Pekinese at a distance of one hundred yards, and at the other, a German shepherd ten feet away. Peter is confronted with the least anxiety-provoking of the stimuli by being asked to imagine the scene while relaxed. After he becomes accustomed to each scene, a slightly more anxiety provoking one is presented until, through repeated trials, he masters the entire hierarchy. The assumption is that the client can not be both relaxed and anxious at the same time. He experiences successively greater tolerance of the feared object until the anxiety is eliminated. This procedure, which also can effectively be carried out in groups, is discussed in more detail in Chapter Ten (see also Wolpe, 1969). (In this procedure care is taken not to eliminate fear of potentially harmful dogs by not presenting scenes such as a German shepherd snarling at someone's knees.)

Regardless of its procedures, behavior modification is characterized primarily by its focus on behavior as the object of change. It is an empirical method in that the counting procedures (monitoring) occur prior, during, and following the application of change procedures in order to test the efficacy of the latter. The behavior modifier does not postulate internal causes of behavior. He does not assume that the behavior is merely a symptom of a deeper, more significant problem; in most cases he assumes that the problematic behavior itself is the problem. Additional problematic behaviors in a client's repertoire must also be dealt with. Symptom substitution is a rare consequence of behavior modification and can be treated like any other behavior (see Bandura, 1969, pp. 50–52).

The procedures of behavior modification are described in this book as they apply within the context of the small group. Although the small group in most cases facilitates use of such procedures, in other cases it may function to limit their effectiveness. The group therapist, therefore, must be informed also of the principles derived from small group theory. Extensive research (see Cartwright and Zander, 1968) concerns the interrelationships among the various attributes of the small group: for example, cohesiveness is related to conformity to group norms; patterns of communication are related to styles of leadership; various structures impinge upon the behavior of individual members in predictable ways. Therefore, if the therapist learns to modify cohesiveness, group norms, and other group structures, he has an added set of tools for modifying his clients' behaviors.

A behavior modification model, unfortunately, does not suggest specific means of utilizing the findings of small group research in the service of behavioral change. Moreover, it has no concepts or operations for dealing with such problems as group composition, group tasks, and phases of group development. For this reason I draw on the concepts of Vinter (1967) in his problem-solving, goal-oriented model of group treatment. He proposes careful assessment not only of the problems of each client in the group but also of social conditions and psychological attributes which might hinder or facilitate treatment. On the basis of this assessment the client is assigned to a group of individuals sufficiently dissimilar to be able to help one another but sufficiently similar to communicate with each other. Also on the basis of the assessment, tentative treatment goals are formulated with the client and group goals are developed with all group members. Once these goals are established, treatment plans are evolved which, being based on research and clinical experience, are believed to facilitate the attainment of treatment and group goals. Treatment plans consist of direct as well as indirect means of intervention. (The former refers to therapist interventions which modify group attributes, such as providing food at all meetings to increase the cohesiveness of the group.) The concept of indirect means of intervention makes the Vinter model especially relevant for group treatment. The goals and intervention procedures are negotiated with the clients, who make a contract agreeing to their respective roles in the process. This contract changes according to the phase and focus of treatment. Goals, assessment, and treatment plans are subject to periodic reevaluation and redesign. In the Vinter model considerable attention is given to the various phases of the group and their implication for the therapist in preparing the group or individual members for the sometimes difficult task of termination.

Group as Context of Change

Since the group is the major context of change and provides a major set of concepts and intervention procedures, let us look briefly at group characteristics which may help or hinder treatment and which distinguish group from dyadic (one client and therapist) treatment. Most authors refer to a group as two or more persons in face-to-face interaction. Since this definition includes dyadic and family treatment it is too general for my purposes. The group as context of treatment in this book refers to a social situation consisting of one or more therapists interacting face-to-face with two or more clients, most of whom are not members of the same family, for the purpose of behavioral, cognitive or attitudinal changes (or all three) in the clients. Since the number of clients in any group usually ranges only from five to eight, this range is assumed in describing the attributes of the treatment group.

In group treatment a client is presented with a wider range of relationships than in dyadic treatment. There are many sources of feedback as to which of his behaviors or attitudes annoy others; he can explore different friendships until he finds his own style; he can try out new forms of communication with others in situations which closely simulate the real world. The group presents a wide range of problems and the client can observe these as well as the procedures, effective and ineffective, which have been utilized to cope with them. As a result of this exposure, he acquires the skills for dealing with new problems—skills that will serve him long after the group has terminated.

In group treatment each client is afforded a possibility of performing leadership or teaching roles for other clients. As he learns treatment procedures, he can demonstrate them to his peers. If he enters the group with skills which are valued by other members, he can teach these to the group; he may be called upon to assist them in achieving the same skills. The group, if sufficiently diverse in membership, in fact provides a variety of models for clients to imitate. (This procedure assumes that most children have at least some behavioral or attitudinal characteristics worthy of emulation.) With this abundance of models the principles of imitative learning can be utilized easily by the therapist.

For most children, the multipeer situation is far more attractive than the therapist-child situation. More activities can be carried out and there are more sources of attention and even affection. There are also more opportunities, when desired, to avoid the imposed intimacy characteristic of two person relationships. As a result of this greater attraction, the pressure to conform to group norms is greater (Cartwright, 1966). When primarily prosocial norms are established in the group, the therapist is afforded the possibility of mobilizing peers as agents of social reinforcement and pressure to change. Using peers as agents of social reinforcement, Patterson and Anderson (1964) demonstrate that significant changes in simple motor responses could be brought about in group treatment. Wahler (1970) programed ten children to serve as behavior modifiers for five of their classroom peers. The latter children (control subjects) were trained to ignore disruptive behavior but give attention to prosocial behavior of the target subjects. As a result there was immediate reduction of disruptive behavior. When the pretreatment condition was reinstated a concomitant rise in disruptive behavior occurred, and when the control subjects resumed extinction the behavior declined sharply again. The group also lends itself to the use of group reinforcement (rewards for the entire group following behavioral accomplishments of the group as a whole, a given subgroup, or even certain specified individuals). Wodarski and his colleagues (1971) demonstrated that group reinforcement is more effective than individual reinforcement in motivating deviant children to conform to therapeutic norms and group goals.

The group also has its limitations. It can become so cohesive that its members spend all their time trying to maintain the group rather than working on their individual or group problems; problems may be denied or ignored for fear of upsetting the tenuous balance in the group. Overcohesiveness can often be dealt with by reinforcing individual performance, by encouraging intragroup competition, and by eliminating group contingencies. Some formalizing of the group program and operating procedures tends to reduce the attractiveness of the group for its members. Occasionally, too, pressures arise in support of a set of maladaptive behaviors, especially during early phases of treatment. Not surprisingly, group attention to such behaviors can circumvent the therapist's efforts to reduce or eliminate the behavior. The power of peer attention in this respect has been documented by Buehler and others (1966) in an institution for delinquent girls. It appeared that the girls received reliable peer approval for antisocial responses but none for prosocial responses, and, as a consequence, high levels of the former responses were maintained. Although this situation can be avoided by carefully monitoring the behaviors of the group members and by controlling other major reinforcers, the therapist must always be aware of the problem.

The group may also be a source of anxiety to those children who lack any social skills. In this case, rather than expecting immediate entrance into the group, a gradual approach may be initiated. The child only looks into the room at first, later attending a meeting for a few minutes without any pressure to participate. Eventually he increases both the time spent at the meeting and the quality and quantity of his participation.

Treatment Phases and Relationships

Thus far I have discussed what the therapist does to achieve change in terms of behavioral and small group procedures, and I have looked briefly at the potential and limitations of the group. An additional tool at the therapist's disposal is his relationship with his clients. In group treatment, as in most therapies, relationship is regarded as a major treatment procedure. But like all variables within a behavioral context, relationship must be operationally defined before it can be observed and dealt with.

Several dimensions of relationship can be operationalized; they have implications for the behaviors of the interacting parties. The first is the degree of personal attraction between individuals; the second is the degree of reciprocity of reinforcement provided. These two characteristics are closely connected. As Stuart (1969) points out, there is extensive empirical support for the proposition that A will be more attracted to B and will reinforce B more if he has been positively reinforced by B. On the basis of this hypothesis, the therapist can increase his attractiveness by increasing his reinforcement of the members as he reduces punishment procedures. Similarly, as the group approaches termination he can reduce his relative attractiveness by helping his clients find social reinforcement outside the group. (Relationship is discussed in more detail in Chapter Twelve.)

The therapist not only alters the nature of the relationship during the course of treatment; almost everything he does is adjusted according to the particular phase of treatment. When all clients begin at approximately the same time, not altogether distinct phases of treatment can be identified: the pregroup phase, in which the therapist collects data to determine the appropriateness of group treatment for each client, as well as the composition of the group; the initial group phase, usually characterized by distribution of high levels of reinforcement; the middle group phase, characterized by its group task orientation; the terminal phase, characterized by emphasis on the transfer of changes; and the follow-up phase, characterized by exploration of the stability and effective transfer of change. In each phase a different contract is negotiated with the client.

In the pregroup phase the therapist interviews the clients and significant adults to determine both the behavioral components of the problem and its concomitant environmental events. He explores potential reinforcers as well as agents of reinforcement and initiates the formation of the group. At this stage the child usually contracts only to see what the group has to offer. In the initial group phase, the therapist gives ample reinforcement, material as well as verbal, merely for attendance in the group; he explores group and individual contracts; tentative treatment plans are initiated, and group cohesiveness is strongly stimulated. The clients contract to do simple behavioral assignments, usually in exchange for potent reinforcement. In this phase, the therapist generally provides a great deal of structure and utilizes client inputs primarily as a form of feedback to evaluate the relevance of his actions.

In the middle phase the therapist begins to shift responsibility to members for their fellow clients' treatment plans. Recreational activities are often faded out, and those that still exist are planned primarily by the clients. The therapist encourages the group to work on determining and monitoring its behavioral assignments, preparing through role-playing to carry them out, and monitoring the completion of and difficulties experienced in previous assignments. Concrete reinforcement for older groups is faded out although praise is still amply used. The client usually contracts to perform difficult assignments and work seriously on his problems. In this phase, the therapist begins to train the clients in responsibility for their own behavior. As they demonstrate skills in this area he gradually shifts decision making to them.

In the terminal phase the therapist fades out most reinforcement, verbal as well as concrete. He focuses on reducing the attractiveness of the therapy group and increasing the attractiveness of alternate groups. Contracts are no longer formally employed. The location and program of meetings are varied, and guests are encouraged to attend. Meetings probably become less frequent until, finally, the group terminates. Those members who need additional help are usually assigned to another group, to an individual therapist for a designated period, or they may even form the nucleus for a new group. In this phase almost all decisions are in the clients' hands. The therapist gives leadership only in focusing clients on termination and transfer of change. In the follow-up phase members are contacted in subgroups or individually. The therapist also contacts parents and teachers to determine whether changes achieved in the group are being maintained. If not, referral for continued treatment is made. Though no formal contract exists in this phase, the former client may agree to help as a model in another group and to contact the therapist if new behavioral problems arise.

Some groups are composed of clients who come as problems arise and go as individual treatment goals are achieved. In these groups the therapist deals with each client, in a sense, in his own treatment phase since one member may just be beginning the group while another is preparing for termination. Although this procedure makes the use of phases difficult for the therapist, it does provide additional models for the entering client and helps him to see readily what he can achieve by the end of treatment.

Why Behavioral Group Treatment?

As pointed out earlier in this chapter, one of the advantages of behavior modification is that it lends itself to evaluation. A therapist not only has data to indicate whether he is successful or unsuccessful at the end of treatment but can observe his relative effectiveness from week to week. Although extensive research demonstrates the procedural effectiveness of the behavior modifier's tools, thus far only a limited amount of research supports the overall effectiveness of behavioral treatment in groups for children. However, additional empirical support for group treatment is to be found in the research related to modification in the classroom and in small, home style treatment units.

Clement and Milne (1967) compared behavioral group treatment and group play therapy to a control group. (See the end of this chapter for a description of play therapy.) In this study eleven eight-year-old, third grade boys, characterized as shy, withdrawn, and anxious, were separated into the three groups mentioned above. The behavioral therapy group, which consisted of four boys who met weekly for fifty minutes, was reinforced with tokens for these previously defined social-approach responses: walking toward another boy or talking to another boy or both. Early in treatment one-word comments were considered "talking," but, later, short phrases were required to receive a token. Accumulated tokens could be used to purchase candy, trinkets, and small toys at the end of the hour. An intermittent schedule of reinforcement was used. The play therapy group received treatment similar to that proposed by Ginott (1961) and commonly carried out in child guidance centers throughout the country. No tokens were administered. The control group met in the therapy room without a therapist for the same fifty minute period. All three groups were observed from behind a one-way mirror and met for fourteen consecutive weeks; mothers' guidance groups were conducted simultaneously. The results of this study showed that the children in the token group improved on the following measures: time spent verbally interacting with one another; time spent playing with one another; degree of proximity to one another; and the behavioral problem check list. The children in the play group improved only by demonstrating a decrease in interaction with adults (assuming less dependency) and in the proximity to other children. There was a significant decrease in social play. In the control group no significant changes were noted.

As the authors point out, the sample was small and there was only one therapist. As a result the study was replicated the following year utilizing a psychoanalytically oriented psychiatrist as therapist and a fourth category: no group, no treatment control. Although at the time the article was written only preliminary data were available, the behavioral therapy group showed by far the greatest improvement and the play therapy group showed the greatest deterioration (Clement, Fazzone, and Goldstein, 1970).

Two of the major side effects noted were that attendance in the token group was much better than in the other groups and the affect of the boys to the therapist was much more positive in the behavioral therapy than in the play therapy group. The therapist also noted that he felt more relaxed and effective in the behavior therapy group because he was having an impact on the children he was trying to help.

Additional support for a behavioral approach to group treatment is to be found in a study by Hinds and Roehlke (1970), who tested the following hypotheses: Group counseling which uses a learning theory approach is effective in modifying specific problem behaviors in elementary school children within the counseling situation; behaviors modified in the counseling situation transfer to the classroom situation. Forty third, fourth, and fifth grade children referred by their teachers because of behaviors which interfered with classroom learning were assigned to four experimental groups and a control group. Each group met biweekly with a male and female counselor for ten weeks. Counseling with the experimental groups involved the use of systematic reinforcement to shape each child's behavior toward the adaptive responses selected for him and to reduce his interfering responses. The program was the same for the control group except that systematic extinction and reinforcement procedures were not introduced. The results indicated that the experimental groups were significantly more effective than was the control group in effecting change and transferring that change to the classroom; they lend support to both hypotheses and to the value of a behavioral approach to group treatment.

Additional research support for behavioral group treatment is found in studies on behavioral change in the classroom. Barrish, Saunders, and Wolf (1969) developed a classroom token program aimed at eliminating disruptive behavior. The class was divided into two teams, and for appropriate behavior each child earned points which were accumulated for rewards shared by all team members. Privileges earned were extra recess, first to line up for lunch, extra projects, and so forth. This project made interesting use of intergroup competition. In another study (Schmidt and Ulrich, 1969), a group control procedure for suppression of excessive classroom noise was utilized. The noise level was monitored on a decible meter. Reinforcement, which consisted of a two minute addition to the class gym period, was given for successively lower noise levels in the classroom.

In the studies mentioned thus far, the behaviors treated are primarily concerned with the client's relationship to classmates and other peers. Specifically, the focus is on such problems as reducing the frequency of aggressive behavior; increasing ways of approaching peers and making friends; and decreasing the frequency of whining, complaining, wheedling, and other maladaptive verbal behaviors.

Attention in group treatment is also given to reducing common but not necessarily interactive behaviors such as glue-sniffing, stealing, and overeating, as well as increasing work and school skills. Of concern to some group members are primarily individual problems, such as generalized anxiety, phobias, and compulsions, which may have been located by group means. Although these have only occasionally been explicit targets of change, anxiety reduction in particular appears to be a major side effect of gaining control of the behaviors mentioned above.

The behavioral parameter of treatment is in part a function of the age parameter. Though many aspects of this approach can be and are used with adult groups, the examples in this book are drawn entirely from children's groups. Children as young as four and as old as sixteen have been treated behaviorally in groups using most of the methods already described. In the older groups, however, the focus is on the use of models, behavioral rehearsal, and behavioral assignments. Reinforcement is primarily in the form of praise and group rewards—for example, providing the entire group with activity or other kinds of rewards for completion of a common task or set of tasks. Moreover, even group reinforcement is faded early in treatment. Also in the older age range attention must be given to clarifying the purpose of the group and the mutual expectations of staff and client and to involving the clients completely early in treatment.

Sponsors and Settings

Though not all social agencies provide treatment facilities for children, the examples in this book are drawn from a broad sample of education, recreation, and welfare services. The youngest children's groups were organized under the auspices of nursery school and Head Start programs, and a large number of groups were organized in elementary and junior high schools. Although most groups met after school or during official breaks such as lunch or recess, some groups met during classtime. Group behavior therapy has been sponsored by community centers and settlement houses. One settlement house used the groups as the basis of a predelinquency project (see Rose, Sundel, Delange, Corwin, and Palumbo, 1970). Also the typical psychiatric services such as mental health and child guidance clinics have been experimenting with behaviorally focused small groups. This approach has also been established in correctional institutions and small treatment homes (Phillips, 1968; Rose, Flanagan, and Brierton, 1971b), where groups are used to train children in behaviors needed to adapt to the institution or negotiate the demands of the outside world. Regardless of the sponsoring agency, the setting for treatment has varied considerably. Groups have met not only in the schools and agencies mentioned but also in stores, clients' homes, hamburger joints, homemade clubhouses, station wagons, and so forth. The principles involved are twofold: simulate as nearly as possible the setting in which the problems occur, and find as attractive a setting as possible to increase the attractiveness of the group.

The reader has now been presented with the basic assumptions of and empirical support for a behavioral approach to group treatment. He is acquainted with the problems on which it is focused and some of the procedures for change as well as the relevance to the process of the group and the agency setting in which the problems occur. But this is not the only model for therapy with children. Of the other models, in fact, two, play therapy and activity therapy, are more widely used.

Other Group Therapies for Children

Play therapy in groups (Ginott, 1961, 1968) is probably the most prevalent group treatment in psychiatric services throughout the country. This therapy, designed for children from three to nine years, aims, like all analytical therapies, at bringing about permanent personality changes. The basic assumption is that children modify their behavior in exchange for adult acceptance. In addition to a physical setting which provides an abundance of toys, the major tools are similar to those of other psychotherapies: establishment of a therapeutic relationship, evocation of catharsis, development of insight, testing of reality, and development of sublimation. The focus of treatment is on the individual: no group goals are established, nor is group cohesiveness encouraged. Nevertheless, the group provides a child with vicarious catharsis; that is, he can observe others doing the things he would like to do (Ginott, 1968). In group therapy a child is forced to evaluate his behavior and personality in light of peer reactions rather than interpretations. He is forced to test himself in relation to the social actualities of the group setting.

The role of the therapist is generally permissive; this permissiveness engenders regressive behavior in children, which Ginot considers a necessary stage of the child's recovery process. However, unrestricted acceptance of behavior is not implied.

The therapist limits acts which are not accepted in society—such as highly destructive acting out behavior—but in play with dolls or other toys, he permits the free expression of destructive feelings and behaviors which symbolize the most forbidden acts (for example, incest and murder).

Activity group therapy usually focuses on eight- to twelve-year-olds (Slavson, 1955). It is a form of ego therapy which aims at treating behavior and character disorders but not psychosis or intense psychoneurosis. In groups of five to eight, boys or girls of similar social-physical characteristics but dissimilar presenting problems meet weekly for two hours in a large room well provided with materials for arts and crafts and for individual and group games. The therapist is essentially neutral and permissive, neither assigning tasks nor setting limits as is done in play therapy. Treatment prescribes not so much what the therapist should do but how he should be. As a passive participant he observes and attempts to understand the underlying meaning of everything the child does. He conveys an image of strength, calm, friendliness, and tolerance even in the face of frustration. His major function is to serve as a model for identification. For example, at the end of a therapy session the therapist begins to clean up himself rather than telling the children to clean up. Slavson gives little attention to the group itself as a means of treatment. The regression which he claims it stimulates is seen as a handicap to be overcome, and the group with minor exceptions appears to be merely a convenient context for therapy.

The major problem with both these approaches is that they do not readily lend themselves to evaluation. Since goals are rarely set, it is not clear what has been achieved or whether permanent personality change has been brought about. Another problem is the use of vague concepts which are difficult to operationalize and about which there appears to be limited agreement. As a result, prescriptions to the therapist are general and ill-defined, and training is often restricted to developing therapist attributes. Although the group is held in higher esteem in play therapy, neither method makes any great attempt to incorporate the available knowledge about small groups. And in both methods there appears to be little system to the therapist's approach. Indeed, the fear is that the therapist might somehow superimpose his values on the children.

For their part, the proponents of these approaches are often critical of behavioral methods. They accuse those who use it of being manipulative, of dealing with irrelevant symptoms, of imposition of adult values, of being undemocratic, and of ignoring the relevance of relationship and feelings. These and other criticisms are dealt with in the course of this book, and, for a detailed discussion of the issues, the reader is referred to Breger and McGaugh (1965) and Kanfer (1965).

2

Composing the Group

The therapist received an urgent call from the third grade teacher. Seven of her oldest boys were constantly fighting, bickering, name-calling, and even stealing. She complained that they were now beginning to influence the rest of the class. Couldn't the therapist put them in one of those groups he was conducting?

During the pregroup phase the therapist usually interviews the client and, depending on the referral source, the parent, teacher, supervisor, parole officer, or other significant persons in the client's life. The purpose of these interviews is to make three basic decisions: Is treatment necessary; is group treatment appropriate; what kind of group would work for the potential client, and how should it be composed? During this period the adults most involved with the problem are usually extremely upset and annoyed with the child. They often want immediate help and many expect immediate change. The child, on his part, is usually upset with the adults. Communication between them has broken down, which has resulted in referral to the sponsoring agency. Information is difficult to obtain since each party blames the other. Nevertheless the therapist attempts to ferret out from each individual involved at least some of the behavioral attributes of the potential client and to zero in on specific incidents in which they are manifested. These interviews are usually brief, focused on precipitating events, and geared toward the behavior pattern of the child and other's reactions to it.

In order to determine whether an individual should be treated at all it is usually necessary to consider the ultimate consequences of his behavior were it to continue. In the third grade class described above the ultimate consequence would have been suspension from or failure in school for the boys involved. One also could not overlook the well-being of the teacher. There are also certain practical considerations in a recommendation for treatment. In the case of a teacher referral, do the parents agree? Are adequate treatment resources available? Is there a danger that treatment will create only an additional handicap if the child, as a result, is labeled "a troublemaker" or "sick"?

As I indicated previously, the group lends itself primarily to the treatment of interactive problems, and, as a rule of thumb, though no empirical evidence about its efficacy exists, at least one of the client's major problems should be in the area of peer or sibling interaction. The reason for this rule is that the group provides an ideal laboratory for trying out new ways of interacting with peers. The therapist can protect the client from the consequences of failure and can control the demands placed on each client as he is learning.

Once each potential group member's problems have been described in a preliminary behavioral statement and a decision has been made that treatment is appropriate, the therapist must decide on a model of composition for the group. Though only limited research exists in this area, we have attempted to develop several models of composition based on it, as well as on recent theory and clinical experience.

Heterogeneous Groups

In examining groups of adults in a mental hospital, Fairweather and others (1964) discovered that heterogeneous groups in terms of degree of chronicity (of psychiatric symptoms) functioned better than homogeneous groups in regard to both productivity and problem focus. On the other hand, in a project concerned with self-control training in groups, Rose, Coles, Flanigan, Sherman, and Flanigan (1970) found no difference between heterogeneous and homogeneous groups. In comparing two groups of smokers and two groups of weight watchers with two groups of mixed composition, the rate of weight loss and reduction of cigarette smoking was the same for homogeneously as for heterogeneously composed groups.

Festinger (1954) points out that when motivated to evaluate their opinions and abilities and when no objective standard exists, people tend to compare themselves to those who are similar rather than different. The implication for grouping is that each individual may differ from the others in some characteristics but that he needs to find someone from whom he is not too distant in terms of high priority characteristics or presenting problem. Lott and Lott (1965), in a review of research findings concerning interpersonal liking, also observe that similarity facilitates communicaton and interpersonal liking.

One might ask whether it would not, on this basis, be ideal to have a group composed entirely of, for example, aggressive children. Clinical experience shows us that groups of this nature indeed become cohesive (high interpersonal liking). However, since the cohesiveness is based on similarities in the very problem areas which the therapist is trying to alter, there is considerable resistance to the therapist and to acceptance of the treatment contract. Research, clinical experience, and social psychological theory suggest, then, a somewhat more complex basis for grouping than similar or dissimilar behavioral manifestations. A set of operations found useful in composing groups according to members' behavioral attributes ranks the behavioral deficits or assets of each client on a scale from 1 to 10 (10 representing a high level). The client then is placed in a group in which at least one other member is near him on most of the continua. For each continuum this may be a different person.

Peter, who is relatively shy, for example, is ranked 2 in assertiveness, 8 in handicraft skills, 3 in study habits, 1 in athletic skills, and 2 (that is, low frequency) in fighting. He is placed in a group with Larry, who is similar in assertiveness, fighting, and athletic skills, and Roger, who has similar skills in handicraft and similar deficits in studying. All members have someone near them in each of the behavioral categories except Tom, who is similar only to Jerry and then only in the fighting category. Though there are some similarities between his and Jerry's profiles, he probably would not be placed in this group. (See Table 1.)

Table 1

	Assertive	Handi-craft	Fighting	Study Habits	Athletic Skills
Peter	2	8	2	3	1
Larry	1	4	1	6	1
Roger	4	6	4	2	4
Jerry	5	4	6	4	3
Tom	9	1	7	1	8

Although there are wide differences among the members along each of the continua, most have some characteristic in common with at least one other person. This similarity affords each person an opportunity to communicate with all other members on some level and, at the same time, learn from them in an area in which he is weak. At times he can be a model or leader and at other times a learner; regardless of the issue, he is rarely an isolate. These rankings are tentative and often difficult to make on the basis of only a few observations and interviews. Continued observation may disclose a totally different pattern. But since a decision must be made before the data are complete, this approach has proven extremely useful. When this procedure is used, one must watch for clustering—the tendency to produce two subgroups at extremes of several of the continua. The cohesive subgroups may severely limit group communication and create subgroup competition.

The groups with which I have dealt range in size from three to eight members. I have found it helpful to begin with a small group and add new members from the second to the fifth week. This allows the old members to explain the group to the new members and, in a sense, to reaffirm the treatment contract by expressing their verbal agreement with it. The groups have been limited to eight members because of the difficulty in developing individualized treatment plans. Larger groups can be handled, however, if all the children share a common problem or if there are two therapists. In most cases, homogeneity in terms of developmental age is useful in order to prevent isolation and to provide a reasonable distribution of communication among the members. Some diversity of physical size and socioeconomic backgrounds can be tolerated and even encouraged where problems are related to social adjustment. It is usually possible to find common activities or tasks in which most of the members have at least minimum skills.

In summary, heterogeneity with respect to behavioral attitudes is recommended for children's treatment groups provided that each child has a "neighbor" in the group along each behavioral continuum. To facilitate communication homogeneity of developmental age is recommended. Diversity in areas such as socioeconomic status has not resulted in serious problems and, in fact, may be advantageous. Other presently employed forms of group composition which have implications for the structure of treatment are summarized below.

Models and Clients Groups

Experiments have been conducted in the schools with groups of four to five children, of whom only one or two have been referred for specific problem behaviors. The nonreferrals serve as behavior models for the others and are aware of their role. The group provides them with opportunities for leadership roles as well as recreational activities. These groups usually last only three to six weeks or until the referred children become able to function in nontherapeutic groups.

The importance of high-status models was demonstrated by Hansen, Niland, and Zandi (1969) in a study of groups of school children from the same socioeconomic class. Using sociometric status as a criterion for group counseling results, the authors divided the class into a group which received reinforcement only, a group which received reinforcement with models, and a control group. The two treatment groups met twice weekly for eight weeks, for the expressed purpose of discussing social behavior in school. In the reinforcement situation, which consisted of low sociometric status students, the interviews were semistructured, the counselor reinforcing ideas, insights, and suggestions relevant to acceptable social behavior. In the model reinforcement situation, interviews were similarly conducted but sociometrically determined high-status persons were added to the group as models. The control students received no counseling but reported to an activity period. Low sociometric students in the model reinforcement group made significantly more gains in social acceptance than did students in the reinforcement and control groups.

Transitional Groups

A guiding principle of treatment groups in correctional institutions has been the achievement of certain behavioral norms prior to qualification of an inmate for the preparole group (for example, Valley View School for Boys, St. Charles, Illinois, in Rose and others, 1971a, 1971b). Since participation in this group is viewed as one of the prerequisites for obtaining parole, admission is highly rewarding. The group focuses on developing behaviors needed to negotiate the family, school, or job situation to which the client plans to return. A furlough usually provides a laboratory for group members to experiment with these new behaviors. Although these groups are often composed of persons with highly diverse behavior problems; the commonality of their goal—leaving the institution—provides solid ground for participation and involvement with others. When problems, status, *and* goals are mixed, the diversity has resulted in a lack of task orientation, disinterest in group goals, and communication problems within the group. For groups other than the preparole group, then, it would be desirable to group according to the continuum principles previously discussed.

Cross-Age Tutor Training Groups

Cross-age tutoring (Lippitt, 1969) is another model for group composition. Clients with classroom problems, especially in the areas of control and study habits, are assigned to tutor younger children with similar problems. The group consists of several tutors who meet to discuss their problems as teachers. The groups are run much more didactically than the model suggested in Chapter One, but most of the same principles could apply. The focus is on teaching the tutors the skills they need to be teachers. One of the major benefits, according to Lippitt (1969), is a growing awareness on the part of the tutor of the problems he is creating for himself, his classmates, and his teachers. In addition, this model puts the client in the novel role of helper; for children with authority figure problems this method appears quite promising.

Natural Groups

The therapist may sometimes be brought in to help natural or previously organized groups. The members may be experiencing a problem among themselves or with the community of which they are a part. (The third graders described earlier are an example of such a group.) In most cases, this group should be treated as a unit, although it may not meet some of the criteria recommended earlier since its most significant problems are usually the interpersonal relationships of the members. Separating them by individual or other group treatment usually makes the problem less accessible. An exception to this recommendation is the natural group or gang whose composition seems to maintain the maladaptive behaviors. A highly cohesive gang of children ranging in age from eight to twenty years was referred by a parole officer to a predelinquency project. The younger members were rapidly learning many delinquent behaviors which were more reinforcing to them than school or socially acceptable recreational activities. The therapist's initial move encouraged breaking the group into age units and integrating the younger children into already existing groups with socially acceptable models and age-appropriate reinforcers.

Errors in group composition can ordinarily be dealt with

without altering the basic composition of the group. In the case of an isolate it may be possible to add a new member or even a new subgroup with similar behavioral attributes; in the case of persistent subgroups, they may be split into two groups and more compatible members added to each. These solutions require a constant source of referrals for group treatment, and when few new clients are available, the therapist may have to explore the alternatives of maintaining the difficult configuration or reshuffling several groups to obtain an effective fit.

The several models discussed here are not exhaustive, and the criteria for choosing any one of them are only suggestive. Further research and experience are required before a definitive decision can be made. The composition of each of these models requires a preliminary assessment of the problem and the child. But, obviously, this is a relatively superficial procedure, and methods for developing the thorough assessment required for later treatment phases are proposed in the following chapters.

3

Behavioral Assessment

Lenny, twelve, was referred to the group by the school counselor because his teacher complained of inattentiveness, manifested by Lenny's habits of staring out the window, sleeping slouched in his chair, and doodling on his notebook. These behaviors occur most frequently during math period but occasionally during other subjects. Whenever the teacher discovers Lenny in these behaviors she yells at him; this, in turn, may maintain his behavior since he appears to get little other attention either from his peers or from the teacher. However, he is also extremely weak in math and as yet has not mastered some of the fundamental skills. Lenny has one friend, Peter, who will also be in the group. Lenny prefers gym to his other subjects and shows some skill in basketball which may serve as a reinforcer for him in improving his paying attention and math skills.

The purpose of assessment is the collection of data and the statement of the problem in such a way that its formulation points to appropriate corrective procedures. As pointed out in the previous chapter, enough preliminary information must be collected to determine whether group treatment is appropriate and to decide group composition. Assessment continues after formation of the group to determine the appropriate targets for change. Most human social patterns may be viewed as voluntary instrumental response patterns or "operants" (Skinner, 1953). The causes of these patterns may be found in the impact of the individual's behavior on the social environment. In order to modify behavior, the therapist must first ascertain the explicit characteristics of the behavior and the explicit environmental events which lead to and maintain both desired and undesired client behaviors.

This chapter discusses the types of behavioral problems which can be dealt with in the small group, specific areas which need to be considered in problem formulation, principles of formulation, and methods of collecting data, both in and out of the group. Appropriate targets of change are primarily those behavioral patterns and deficits which have long-range undesirable consequences for the client or his family. Although special concern in *group* treatment are interactive behaviors (what he does and says to and with others and their responses), the treatment of noninteractive behavior can also be dealt with through the group.

Behavioral Problems

Those behaviors which get the child into trouble at school, with parents, with the police, with prospective employers, or with other members of the community and which in the long run have destructive or otherwise severe aversive consequences for him are called maladaptive behaviors. Since maladaptive behaviors occur with great frequency under certain conditions they are often called "surplus" behaviors (Staats and Staats, 1963). In this category one finds such problems as stealing, lying, fighting with peers, verbal abuse, glue-sniffing, and running away from home. A second category can be defined in terms of behaviors whose absence or low frequency in certain situations has ultimate undesirable results. These behaviors (also called behavioral deficits) are generally adaptive in the given situations and need to be increased in frequency. Examples are infrequent studying, lack of assertive responses, the absence of such verbal skills as asking questions in class, the possession of only one set of recreation skills, or the absence of approach responses.

It is not always easy to determine whether a behavior is adaptive or maladaptive. An adaptive behavior at home may be considered maladaptive in the classroom. The burden of adaptation often falls on the very child whose skills in adaptation are most limited, and the therapist must help him determine the new behaviors he must acquire. The therapist may attempt to modify the demands of teacher or parent or bring about some form of negotiation, but even the best results often require the client, in his low power position, to make the major changes. This dilemma is even more difficult for behaviors designated maladaptive by the police but considered quite adaptive by the client's peers. Under what conditions should the client be taught to adapt to community norms in view of unfavorable consequences from his peers? Generally, the position taken is to facilitate an analysis of the problem to the point where the client can choose the direction he wants to take.

Many problems can be described as either maladaptive behaviors, the frequency of which should be decreased, or adaptive behaviors, the frequency of which should be increased. For example, a school attendance problem may be defined in terms of the number of days absent or the number of days in attendance. Since most of the procedures at our disposal are oriented toward increasing rather than decreasing frequencies, a problem should be defined in terms of adaptive behaviors whenever possible.

Even when a problem must be defined primarily in terms of maladaptive behaviors, it is useful to formulate alternative adaptive behaviors to be performed under the same stimulus conditions. If the child steals in the presence of his older brother when he is bored or annoyed, the therapist should formulate adaptive alternatives such as having the client avoid his brother when he feels annoyed or bored, or teaching him to make verbal responses to the source of his annoyance. For the child who fights excessively with children who call him names, the therapist should formulate adaptive responses to name-calling such as walking away or making verbal expressions of anger.

A third category of problems is behavior which is adaptive under some conditions but maladaptive under others. The client has a problem if he is performing the behavior indiscriminately; that is, without regard to the appropriate circumstances. To a certain degree most problematic behaviors fall into this category, although some more apparently than others. For example, in some neighborhoods aggressive behaviors are required to maintain oneself on the playground but similar behavior will result in expulsion when directed too frequently toward the teacher or peers in the classroom.

A fourth category of problems is inadequate or inappropriate reinforcers. Most children are reinforced by a wide variety of events and objects such as praise, success, or physical activities, as well as primary reinforcers like food. Many children in group treatment respond initially to few reinforcers: food, sexual activities, or automobile riding. A major difficulty can be the absence of any activity within the school which functions as a positive reinforcer. Because of the importance of reinforcement in the outside world as well as in the treatment process, a reinforcement deficit is here discussed separately.

The behaviors so far mentioned are primarily operant behaviors. Groups also lend themselves to the treatment of certain respondent behaviors such as fear or anxiety. A group provides model approach responses which the fearful child can try out with feared objects or events. In groups where most of the clients are fearful or anxious in response to various situations, group desensitization (see Chapter Ten) can be used. Often, however, reinforcement or shaping of approach responses is used instead of desensitization and other respondent procedures.

Improving Instructional Control

Instructions and rules are major regulators of human behavior. To maintain himself in a job, or even in his home, a child must accept a minimum of instructional control. Yet many of our clients only occasionally attend to and still more rarely follow instructions, which may themselves be inadequate, unclear, or excessively demanding. The client may have received little or no encouragement or reinforcement for conforming to instructions in the past. For these reasons his acceptance of instructions has either been extinguished or was never really built into his behavioral repertoire. Nevertheless, clients who are ineffective in this area must be taught how to differentiate among, to attend to, and to follow instructions if they are to survive in normal work and learning situations. Moreover, reinforcement procedures can be greatly enhanced if the client can operate under instructional controls. The goal is not to create a child who is submissive to the whims of all adults (this could not be done, even if that were the intention) but rather to provide the child who rejects all adult mediation with the option of accepting or rejecting it according to the situation at hand.

The degree of control the client has over certain behaviors is also important. A client often wants to stop a behavior but claims he hasn't enough self-control. This includes smoking, sniffing glue, taking drugs, drinking, gambling, lying, and compulsive stealing, which are usually referred to as problems of self-control, although they might be considered problems of inadequate control of the environment. They can be worked with only if the client regards them as problems and indicates a willingness to work on them; under these circumstances, the group is a valuable intermediate form of control and monitoring.

Nonbehavioral Problems

The therapist must also concern himself with the assessment of environmental problems which may be connected to behavior but do not directly involve it. A client is said to have an environmental problem if the conditions in his immediate environment should be changed but he has little or no power to modify them himself (for example, the child who has no shoes to go to school and no socially acceptable means of obtaining them; the child who needs a foster home placement; the teen-age girl who needs legal advice or birth control information). Most statements of the environmental problem must include a description of the perceived need, the availability of services to meet it, the activities of the client and significant others which will be required to attain them, and their importance in terms of ultimate implications for behavioral change. The question as to whether these services should be contingent on behavioral changes will also have to be answered. To what degree can the client participate in obtaining these services? As these questions imply, the distinction between environmental and behavioral problems is not obvious.

Another nonbehavioral area of vital concern is the client's physical condition. The therapist should always question the possibility of poor eyesight or hearing, malnutrition, dysentery, or worms. A physical examination can provide useful information on many clients.

Assessment should not be restricted to the client's problem behaviors but should also describe behaviors he does well. What do people in his environment praise or like him for? What does he seem to enjoy doing? The therapist must likewise determine which of these assets can become a foundation for change. Participating in activities which utilize his behavioral assets may be reinforcing to the client. Finally, if a client's assets include skills which other members of the group do not have, he may more easily be able to assume a teaching or leadership position at some point in treatment. More specifically, the therapist should inquire about athletic skills, intellectual interests or accomplishment, areas of specialized knowledge, craft or mechanical skills, ability in games of any sort, and so forth. "Skill" need not imply expertise and even the simplest ability can be built upon.

Principles of Problem Formulation

It may appear from this description of problems and assets that the therapist, having collected complete information in the first few meetings, initiates treatment in following meetings, and that one follows the other in an orderly sequence. On the contrary, there is constant refining of the problem on the basis of the data continually collected in behavioral treatment. As simple problems are solved, clients tend to volunteer more crucial information, and as the client's nuisance value is reduced in the home and at school, parents and teachers, too, provide more information. Also, of course, as meetings progress, the therapist observes more of the client's interaction patterns within the group.

Assessment, then, may be regarded as an ongoing process which begins with an intake interview and ends when treatment finishes. However, in the initial phases considerably more of the group's and therapist's efforts are spent on data collection although change procedures themselves may begin as early as the first session. Later, as problems become highly specific, the focus shifts to working toward change, to preparation for dealing with future problems, and towards termination of treatment.

The formulation of any problem must begin with a description of the problem behavior, the conditions under which it occurs, and its consequences. In addition, it is necessary to determine those stimuli which are reinforcing and aversive to the client, the agents and forms of reinforcement and punishment, and the nature of any small group, subcultural, or historical variables relevant to the problem description. The foremost principle in formulation is that the statement should focus on behaviors specific enough to be observed. Rather than describing the problem as "dependency," the child is described as one who remains constantly in the proximity of adults, who often asks for help with things most children his age do themselves, and who cries whenever he is refused something he requests. The trait of dependency is difficult to identify; the behaviors mentioned above are more readily seen. Another reason for a high degree of specificity is that for most clients, as well as for their parents or their teachers, observable behavior is of greatest concern. John's mother is upset because he hits his sister, not because he seems to display sibling rivalry.

When Harold runs around in class, it is not his underdeveloped superego structure or lack of self-esteem that prevent the teacher from teaching.

Another reason for specificity is that many change procedures are available for modifying specific behavioral manifestations whereas there are very few explicit procedures for dealing with more general diagnostic categories. Moreover, behavior which is readily observable can likewise be readily monitored or counted (see Chapter Four). Because changes in frequency provide an ongoing basis for evaluation of success or failure, whenever possible the problematic behavior is also described in terms of its relative frequency. For example, Anne runs away about once a month for a period of two or three days; Jack gets into two or three fights a day; Harry follows only two of the ten instructions given him during the week.

Not only can traits or other internal phenomena be reduced to a more concrete level, but behavior which at first seems relatively specific can also be broken down. For example, a problem such as irregular school attendance is probably more accurately described as a set of problems: lack of reading skills, lack of studying skills, high frequency of delinquent street games (the pay-off for which is higher than that for school attendance), and lack of reinforcers in the school situation. A problem such as frequent loss of job, even though the client wants to work, may often be broken down into such behaviors as the following: anxiety responses like hand tremors and avoidance of eye contact in the presence of strange adults; absence of verbal skills; and avoidance of new situations. Disobedience may consist of lack of attending behaviors and an excess of day dreaming. In fact, when a parent or teacher complains of disobedience, the therapist should help them focus on what the client is not doing that he should be doing, regardless of whether or not he was asked to do it.

Although the environmental response or consequence of a behavior problem is surely relevant to its description, the problem should be defined primarily in terms of the client's behavior, not in terms of the environmental response. "He annoys his parents" is not a correct behavioral definition of a problem. "He teases the dog, scatters his clothes around the room, whines when asked to do chores," is. His parents' annoyance is one assumed consequence of these behaviors.

Similarly, a problem is not behaviorally defined when defined solely in terms of a lack of desired resources such as money, recreational equipment, or even friends. This does not imply that the therapist will not try to facilitate obtaining these resources. But if the client can play a role in obtaining them, it is essential first to define those behaviors which presently interfere with this. For example, in the case of the child who has no friends, the problem must be defined in terms of the behaviors he must learn or unlearn in order to obtain friends and keep them. The therapist cannot give him a friend; he can only be taught to perform in such a way that he is more likely to make friends and be helped to explore social situations in which he is likely to meet them. Most general problems which are modifiable by the therapist can be redefined in this way. Several exceptions (noted earlier in this chapter) involve helping the client to obtain resources which his present behaviors prevent.

In describing a client's behavior the use of the words "able," "willing," "unwilling," implies judgments which can seldom be justified by the data. To avoid this error, these words, their cognates, and similar words implying capacity or motivation are rarely used in the behavioral statement of a problem. A statement like "Frank cannot listen to his parents" becomes "Frank does not attend [listen] to parents, as evidenced by absence of eye contact, frequent requests to repeat what they have said, and noncompliance with their demands."

Environment Surrounding Behavior

When describing the core of the problem, the emphasis is on the client's behavior. The problem is incomplete, however, without a description of its environmental context, which consists of those events concurrent with and immediately antecedent to the problematic behavior. These conditions are referred to as the stimulus conditions or discriminative stimuli (S^d). The context is relevant insofar as it provides the necessary or alternate (but not sufficient) conditions for the behavior to occur. Normally, the conditions are neither necessary nor sufficient, but their presence indicates a high probability that the given behavior will take place: On sunny days (event 1), when Peter asks Johnny to "take off" (event 2), especially after Johnny has argued with his mother (event 3), Johnny truants from school. These conditions often point to ways of bringing about change. Although there may not be much one can do about the weather (except to be watchful on nice days), one can teach mother and/or Johnny to develop new decision-making skills or to find new ways of responding when the other disagrees. One might also help Johnny create more positive interactions with Peter or other friends.

The stimulus conditions may be taken into account in defining whether a given behavior is adaptive or maladaptive. Running in the playground is adaptive; in the school classroom or corridor it is maladaptive. When refused something by a friend, loud assertive behavior may be adaptive, but it probably is not if refused something by the principal. Specific treatment procedures thus can be designed to help the client distinguish between situations in which a behavior is appropriate or inappropriate.

Like problem descriptions, stimulus descriptions must be of specific and observable conditions. The italics below show examples: *When Bobby has no money* and is *in the company of Chuck,* he breaks into vending machines; *when Lydia appears tired (eyes are red and half closed; movements are slow and listless),* and *when grandmother or auntie is present,* Lydia whines or cries and makes demands for presents. In most cases the stimulus conditions which evoke the behavior occur immediately prior to it; the further in time from the behavioral event, the more hypothetical the relationship. The reader should note also that there is usually a series of stimulus conditions under which the problematic behavior occurs. Frequently, when any one of the preconditions is not present, the behavior will not occur. In the first example above, if Bobby could either be given some spending money or helped to avoid Chuck, the likelihood of his stealing might be greatly decreased. Since some treatment procedures aim at modifying the stimulus conditions, these must be clearly distinguished and specified in the problem formulation.

A number of types of stimulus conditions exist. Some stimuli evoke the given behavior; for example, "I dare you to hit me!" is an evoking stimulus for some children. Other stimuli tend to create conditions which increase the likelihood of the behavior. Some stimuli (for maladaptive as well as for adaptive behaviors) are internal, such as hunger or sexual stimulation. But even in these cases, it is necessary to specify the overt indications (for example, verbal statements). In the examples given, one finds both human (Chuck) and physical (fatigue) stimuli leading to problematic behavior. In one example, the absence of stimuli (spending money) and the presence of an available object might function as stimulus conditions for the maladaptive behavior of stealing.

Determining Reinforcers

Most behavior is followed by the occurrence of certain events or the presence of certain objects in the environment, many of which are consequences of the given behavior. Most consequences are immediate but some may be delayed; more immediate consequences tend to have far more impact on the future occurrence of the behavior. Those consequences which increase the probability of a future occurrence of the preceding behaviors are called positive reinforcers; and those consequences which, when removed, increase the probability of a future occurrence are called negative reinforcers. When the teacher leaves the room, Albert runs around while the other children laugh. Their laughter serves as a positive reinforcer if it increases the likelihood that Albert will run again under similar circumstances.

Marcia is watching TV; as her mother nags her, Marcia turns up the volume on the set, and mother leaves angrily. The withdrawal of nagging functions as a negative reinforcer for Marcia's volume adjustment, since under the same conditions, she will probably turn up the volume again. Since the major treatment procedures used in this approach involve the presentation or removal of reinforcers, the consequences of any given behavior should be determined as early as possible. It is also important to ascertain how maladaptive behaviors are presently being maintained. Generally, an analysis of the sequence of events (the discriminative stimuli, the maladaptive behavior, and the immediate consequences) will suggest what parents, teachers, peers, or the individual himself may be doing to evoke and maintain the behavior.

If the problem is one of absence or low frequency of adaptive behaviors, the therapist attempts to ascertain what consequences seem to be maintaining adaptive behaviors already in the client's repertoire; in this way he can reasonably predict what environmental events might reinforce a new or infrequent behavior. For example, Augie, eleven, rarely studies, seldom does chores for his parents, and has few interests. The one thing he does well is running errands for his grandfather. After close examination, it appears that grandpa is the only one who tells him a story; and there is a story if and only if Augie runs the errand. It thus becomes apparent that either the stories or the total attention of an adult might be used to reinforce adaptive school behaviors, chore behaviors, or desirable social behaviors.

When adaptive behaviors are being maintained, one can explore what events or stimuli are or may be reinforcing to the client by showing him a reinforcement menu (Daley, 1969), on which he ranks each item according to its attractiveness. One can also, of course, observe the activities for which he shows a preference and hypothesize that his interests will be somewhat dictated by the sociological taste pattern of his peer group and his subculture.

A list of potential reinforcers is usually insufficient, however, and some effort should be made to determine their relative priority for each client. Since deprivation of highly attractive experiences or objects increases their effectiveness as reinforcers (Staats and Staats, 1963, p. 309), the therapist should also determine which reinforcers are available and which are lacking in his client's natural environment. For example, when one therapist discovered that his resistive but "hotrod-happy" clients had no access to vehicles, he used minutes of driving time of the agency's car as an effective change procedure.

Consequences can also be used to decrease the frequency of or eliminate a maladaptive behavior. Two of the most frequently used are the presentation of negative reinforcers (or aversive stimuli) and the withdrawal of positive reinforcement. (These and other procedures for reducing the frequency of behavior are discussed in detail in Chapter Seven.) Both are regarded as acts of punishment. Although punishment may result in undesirable side effects, it is often an effective control procedure. The therapist needs to explore the types of punishment the child receives, their frequency, their effectiveness as a means of control, and any unpredicted responses to them such as emotional side effects, avoidance of the punisher or punished situation, or uncontrolled anger. Events which would function as punishment for most children serve as reinforcement for some. That is, the behavior which the adult assumes he is punishing tends to increase following the "punishment." This may result from a deficit of attention obtained in any other way, because of sexual satisfaction derived from the act of punishment, or because the immediate reinforcement far offsets the effect of the delayed punishment. For this reason it is important to discover whether "punishment" does indeed function as such for the client.

Although my approach is primarly based on positive reinforcement, punishment procedures may be utilized under certain conditions (see Chapter Eight). If this is the case, careful analysis of the punishment practices of significant others as well as the events which function as aversive stimuli is called for.

Assessing Complex Behaviors

Problems have thus far been considered solely as isolated units involving discriminative stimuli, the given behavior, and its consequences. Often, however, problem behaviors are part of a cycle of events. For example, Henrietta was referred for running away from home. Her running away was usually preceded by an argument with her father which in turn was preceded by her spending too much money or dressing "too flimsily." Since father provides the money in the first place—whenever he feel like it but especially when she returns from running away—this precedes her overspending. Examining this cycle of events, it becomes apparent that there are multiple points of intervention: Henrietta may be taught to respond differently to father's anger; father may be taught to respond differently to Henrietta's running away; and Henrietta may be taught to use her money more wisely or to avoid arguments with her father. Analysis of the cycle can frequently relate a number of problems which might otherwise have been dealt with as a series of isolate behaviors.

Since assessment often involves more than one problem, the therapist must determine the priority. An important consideration at this point is the societal consequences of each problem. "If he doesn't stop fighting with knives or chains, he will be sent to the correctional school the next time he is caught." "If he continues to miss school at the present rate, he will be expelled within two weeks." In both examples the long range consequences are such that either problem would have priority over, for example, the low frequency of chore behaviors at home. The "nuisance value" of a behavior should also be considered. If the teacher is frantic because her class is being disrupted, and the mother upset because her favorite glassware is being destroyed, these behaviors may be the therapist's primary target. "Nuisance value," moreover, is seldom separate from long range aversive consequences.

Ayllon and Azrin (1968a, p. 49) point out an equally valid consideration when ranking problems for treatment: "Teach only those behaviors which will continue to be reinforced after training." There is little point in eliminating a behavior during treatment which will be encouraged later by teachers, parents, or peers. In fact, the client may be punished by any of these individuals if he returns to them without his previously "normal" and expected behavior.

Determining Who Reinforces

In order to ascertain whether a behavior will be reinforced or ignored outside the group, the therapist must discover which persons control the major positive and negative reinforcers in a client's environments. They are often peers who are more delinquent or "disturbed" than he is and not the adults who provide him with his basic necessities. In the classroom, for example, classmates' responses are often more highly valued than the teacher's. Neither can the material aspect of the reinforcing event be separated from the person who delivers it. The ten dollars which a client receives from his father may not reinforce the behavior which preceded his father's gift, but the same client may be strongly reinforced by the quarter which his uncle gives him. Once the chief agents of reinforcement have been determined, it is sometimes possible to include them in the treatment plan. If these are the client's peers, the case for group treatment is strong.

Most families and teachers do use reinforcement procedures to control and educate the children with whom they live or work. When the procedures are ineffective, there are usually fundamental errors in the method of delivery. In the early analysis of the problem it is therefore important to explore how the client is being reinforced. Is reinforcement administered consistently? What is the schedule of reinforcement? Is its administration arbitrary or are there well-defined criteria for giving or withdrawing it? If such data are studied, the therapist can often discover ways to program well-meaning but inefficient "significant-others" to treat the child, and such "treatment" can be extremely beneficial when carried out simultaneously with the group programs.

Collecting Data Through Discussion

Also of concern to the behavioral therapist is the means of collecting data. How this information may be obtained from relevant adults is discussed in part in Chapter Fifteen. The means of gaining information from the clients during group meetings, however, involves reinforcement for and shaping of problem-focused talk. Briefly, tokens are first given for anything which vaguely resembles such talk; gradually the therapist shapes discussion of specific problematic behaviors and their stimulus and consequent conditions by rewarding successively more specific statements. He promotes group discussion through direct questions and prompting. (Shaping will be discussed more fully in Chapter Seven.) In the following example the therapist meets with his group for the first time. The group was chaotic; members were running around the room, screaming, and fighting. The therapist asked them to sit down at the table. Only Johnny approached the table. The therapist gave Johnny a small candy. Pete shouted from across the room, "Don't I get one?" The therapist sat quietly; Pete came to the table. The therapist continued to sit quietly; Pete sat down. The therapist began to tell them about the group. "Why don't we get candy?" Aaron asked. "You didn't earn it," the therapist replied. "This is a fun group but you have to work in order to earn, just like your fathers." "What's the purpose of this group?" the therapist asked. "To have fun," Aaron replied. "Good," said the therapist, giving him a candy. "What else did we discuss when I talked to each of you alone?" (Note that the therapist provides cues for the responses, which will be rewarded.) "To help us get along better in school?" shouted Ed and Phillip at the same time. "Good!" said the therapist, passing out a candy to each. The discussion immediately zeroed in on problems they were having in school. The therapist continued to pass out candies immediately following problem-oriented responses.

In addition to using reinforcement in the group to obtain information from the clients, there are a number of other data sources available to the therapist. He can interview the client and his significant adults individually. He can observe the client not only in the group but, if necessary, in the classroom, on the playground, and at home. However, because many clients lack sufficient verbal skills to describe the various components of their problems and observations at crucial moments may be impossible, role playing is often used to facilitate data gathering. Many clients can reveal the details of their problems when asked to "play" themselves in specific situations.

In the following example Jerry demonstrates how he got in trouble on the playground. His teacher claims that Jerry's fighting is a problem; Jerry blames it on the other person.

Therapist: Ok, I'm the playground teacher. Jerry and Tom, you play yourselves, and Allen, you play the guy that Jerry tried to sock. How did it start, Jerry?
Jerry: Me and Tom are playing catch, when this other guy comes along and wants to butt in.
Therapist: Ok, let's play it. Throw the ball back and forth.
Tom and Jerry: (Throw ball back and forth.)
Allen: Hey guys, let me in. Toss me the ball.
Jerry: (Viciously) Get lost, man.
Tom: (Under his breath) Give it to 'em, Jerry!
Allen: Why not? C'mon be a sport, toss it.
Jerry: I said get lost, or I'm gonna sock you.
Tom: (Softly) Sock 'em, Jerry!
Therapist: Hey, what's happening there?
Jerry: This bum's trying to move in on us.
Tom: Yeah!

It quickly becomes clear that the provoking behavior of the third boy was extremely mild and that Tom served as the major stimulus for Jerry to fight. Moreover, Tom's applause was maintaining the behavior.

Throughout this chapter I have stressed the importance of specificity in describing problem behaviors and the conditions surrounding them. In the last section I suggest a method of determining general categories about behavior and its environment; in the following chapter I discuss more precise methods of data collection.

4

Monitoring and Charting

According to the group members' teacher, only one incident of talking back occurred last week.

The therapist observed that Red spoke up three times and Dennis twice during the hour-and-a-half meeting.

According to their parents all of the boys obeyed curfew for the week, which Tom recorded, amid applause, on the group chart.

Barry showed the therapist the result of his five math assignments, all of which he had completed on time. This brought his chart up to a total of fifty-two math assignments completed in the past two months.

Billy reported that Alex either teased or shoved Robbie three times last week. Alex said it was twice and Robbie thought it was four times, so the therapist recorded an average of three times on Alex's chart which was two less than the previous week.

In all of these examples, individual or group behaviors are being counted. Counting or other forms of behavior measurement are referred to as monitoring, an essential step in the change process. Without monitoring, effective behavioral treatment is almost impossible. If no means of counting a behavior can be devised, this is usually an indication that the behavior has not been specifically defined. Monitoring provides the client and therapist with an estimate of the client's achievements at all points during treatment, and is a relatively clear indication when treatment is not succeeding and needs to be altered.

At the onset of monitoring and charting, therapists often discover an apparent reduction of maladaptive and an increase of adaptive behaviors. The change is "apparent" since, prior to monitoring, there is only a rough estimate of frequency. But most teachers and parents are surprised by what they perceive to be "improvement" even before other change procedures have been introduced. Monitoring a maladaptive behavior is usually mildly aversive since it is a way of pointing out that the child has done something wrong one more time. Monitoring of adaptive behavior, on the other hand, often serves as a form of approval since it is a way of pointing out that the child has done something correct or good one more time. Hence, clients are reinforced for the adaptive behavior.

Individual or group charts on which to record data derived by monitoring provide the participants with a comparative picture of the course their treatment is taking and represent a summary of the monitoring results. Although in practice monitoring and charting are not distinguished, for purposes of analysis I shall discuss them separately.

Self-Monitoring

In the previous examples the counting was carried out by the client, by his peers, by the therapist, by observers or aides, by teachers, and by parents. Each has a unique contribution in the monitoring process and each presents a unique bias. In the early phases of treatment, a client may be asked to observe his own behavior in order to determine his problem, but he is seldom asked to count the behavior systematically. The major problem with this is that the client may be trained in "lying" behavior if the therapist reinforces verbal descriptions of desirable change; that is, the client will increase verbal accounts of desirable performance since the verbal description is reinforced. In the beginning of treatment, moreover, most clients lack the skills and discipline required to monitor. In most cases, however, the client becomes at some point the sole or major monitor of his own behavior. This occurs when he has clearly demonstrated to himself that improvement per se is reinforcing. Until that time he may nevertheless monitor himself, provided that there is an explicit validating source (parent, teacher, other group member). Early forms of self-monitoring involve broad descriptions of problems the client encounters in carrying out his assignments. There is usually no reinforcement for these descriptions (except when "problem-talk" is being encouraged) in order to avoid undesirable verbal habits. Certain phenomena are not readily accessible to anyone but the client and one of the advantages of self-monitoring, certainly, is that it makes these phenomena accessible to treatment. However, for children whose phobias are the major presenting problem, it is usually better to deal with observable avoidance behaviors rather than internalized fear responses.

Therapist as Monitor

The therapist normally can monitor only those behaviors which occur in the group. Although some group behaviors are extremely relevant, the brief weekly periods are such a small sample of the client's life that monitoring of outside behavior is essential to the validation of in-group changes and a determination of how well these changes have generalized to other situations. One of the advantages of the therapist as monitor is that monitoring is then viewed by the client as a central part of the treatment. Moreover, the therapist provides himself as a model in the counting process—a first step in training the client in self–monitoring. Immediate feedback on ongoing changes in the group is available to the therapist—if maladaptive behaviors are increasing and adaptive ones decreasing, he knows immediately that what he has been doing is at best ineffective and possibly detrimental and has a basis for change. It is difficult, however, for the therapist to observe more than one client at a time. Some therapists have met this problem by using counters (one for each behavior) but unless the therapist is well organized and the behavior highly specific, it is difficult to both monitor and run the meeting. Others use brief time-samples to observe different pairs of children in the meeting and still others use observers who watch the group either from behind a one-way mirror or from the side-lines. However, if the observer is restricted to an observation room, the group can be observed only in a limited setting and if the observer roams with the group, he can not avoid interacting with the members and in so doing may limit the objectivity of the data. Nevertheless, observers are probably more objective than the therapist, the parent, or the client himself, all of whom have much more at stake in the treatment process. To offset the increased cost of treatment necessitated by additional staff, volunteers who want to observe behavioral treatment have been successfully recruited as observers.

An extremely useful procedure for slowing down the interaction so that careful group observations can be made by the therapist or observers is called the "freeze" technique (see Blackham and Silberman, 1971). The therapist sets a kitchen timer at a given or random interval. The children are instructed to "freeze" when the bell goes off; that is, hold whatever position they are in. The therapist monitors such behaviors as "out of seat," physical contact with another, eye contact with him, withdrawn behavior, as well as movement by children who fail to freeze. This is also an excellent technique for teachers, who have an even greater problem observing behavior without interrupting their teaching.

Parents, Teachers, and Peers as Monitors

The major problem with such monitoring is the limited setting, which is one reason parent and teacher monitoring are frequently used as additional sources of information. Provided clear guidelines and a limited number of observations are requested, parents and teachers will often count at least those behaviors which are a nuisance to them. In most cases parents are quite ready to note or to count temper tantrums, fights with siblings, complaining, whining, completion of household chores, time child arrives home, time child goes to bed, and similar discrete behaviors. Teachers have shown readiness to count out-of-seat behavior, talking at inappropriate moments, swearing, and a variety of academic behaviors, although training in or demonstration of counting procedures or both may also be necessary.

Communications from the therapist to the parent or teacher and vice versa may be carried by the client and can be explicit forms with blanks for the monitor to fill in. (Prior to giving the child the message, the therapist should contact the parent or teacher to explain how the data is to be collected.)

> Nancy has complimented her sister ____________ times this week. Nancy has fought with her sister while either parent was present ____ times this week (April 7–14).
>
> ____________ ____________________
>
> Date Parent's Signature

As might be expected, some clients will forge names or change the data and, in rare cases, parents will collaborate with the child to present a false picture. However, these problems are infrequent and the children usually admit the deception if confronted with it. Random inquiries by the therapist by telephone or through personal contact with the teacher or parent usually decrease the likelihood of fraud. The members are, of course, aware that such checks are made from time to time.

Group members frequently can be trained to monitor

one another. Obviously, peers see each other in situations which no adult observes; such situations are especially significant if peer-relations is the client's problem area. In spite of its potential value, however, training child-clients as monitors has proven no easy task. The major problem is that most clients lack the discipline which such observation requires. And the "no tattling" or "squealing" norm which prevails in youth groups discourages many clients. Nevertheless, after extensive training, clients have successfully observed each other in such behaviors as fighting, teasing, and whining. In all cases the observed client agreed to and helped plan the conditions for observations, and helped train his peer observer. Participation by the observed client greatly reduces the onus on client monitors.

An interesting observation procedure for children, especially in large groups, is the use of an inner and outer circle. Half the clients sit in an inner circle and the other half behind them in an outer circle. Each member in the inner circle is observed at an on-going task by one member in the outer circle. This procedure is usually employed for monitoring such behaviors as participation, use of "putdowns," manifestation of specified leadership behaviors, subgrouping, task-oriented talk, disruptive comments, and giggling. Group members can also be trained in observational skill with this technique.

Regardless of who does the monitoring, it is not an easy process. "Running away from home," for example, seems at first glance an easy behavior to measure. But how far must a child go and for how long must he be away before it is "running away"? What if he threatens to run away but merely hides in the back seat of the family car? Before a behavior can be counted it must be clearly defined in terms of duration, intensity, and so forth. The test of a good formulation is whether or not it can be counted and for this reason assessment is closely linked to monitoring.

Sampling Procedures

It is impossible to observe a behavior twenty-four hours a day and/or everywhere the child goes. A rational sampling system must be developed regardless of the monitor and the monitored behavior. A behavior such as "coming home after 10 p.m." indicates in its very formulation the time and place for observation. Behaviors which are neither time nor place specific in formulation must be made so before sampling can be done. For example, Henry fights with his younger brothers. After finding out what actions constitute a "fight," the monitor must observe when and where these occur. He will then try to be at the place where fights usually occur at high frequencies. There may be other fights but since mother cannot be everywhere all the time, this is a sampling error one must accept. It is important that parents do not give up cooperating in the monitoring process simply because their instructions are too general or because excessive demands for observation have been made. A rule of thumb as to the length of the sample is that the less frequent the behavior the longer the time sample. For example, if tantrums occur twice a day, the sample would consist of the entire waking day. If tantrums occurred several times an hour, two or three randomly selected hours might be sufficient. If nail biting occurred almost constantly, one half hour a night might provide a sufficiently large sample.

No reference has been made to discrepancies in the amount of time from day to day during which observation can be made. If one observes fighting with peers one hour a day on Tuesday and two hours on Wednesday, any increase is probably a function of the observation system and not of a change in behavior. For this reason, it is often preferable to estimate the rate per hour or per minute rather than the absolute number per hour or even per week. Even when the observation periods are roughly comparable, it is usually helpful to bear in mind this estimated rate in the event that at some time the observation period will have to be altered. In order to calculate the rate, one need only know the length of the period during which the client was observed and the frequency of the observed behavior.

Recording Data

Most counting is done by hand during a specified period. Tally charts are designed in advance and put (with a pencil) in a readily accessible place. For example, every time the child is seen fighting with his sister, regardless of who initiates it, a stroke is made on the chart. Most charts also indicate when behavior is to be observed and a space for comments is helpful, especially when refining the definition of the problem behavior during the early phase of treatment. My experience shows that if tabulation charts are prepared in advance, parents or teachers are more likely to count accurately than when they must only note the data on a blank piece of paper. Moreover, if time is available, the charts are first designed with the parent or teacher, and frequently the child, before the therapist works out a final copy. These are not the only ways of tabulating data; a common procedure is to use a calendar page pasted on a piece of cardboard and tacked in a prominent place. The data can be recorded over the printed numbers.

An example of a group tally sheet is illustrated in Table 2. This is a common way of keeping track of a number of behaviors for a number of boys at the same time, and allows for differential reinforcement systems and for response costs (subtracting points for certain behaviors). It provides a quick overview of each member's progress and can often eliminate the need for further charting.

The use of a hand counter (Lindsley, 1968), rather than tallies or check lists, is a fairly effective means of monitoring certain high-frequency behaviors if the boundaries of the behavior are well defined. A stopwatch is used frequently to record the number of minutes of such behaviors as out-of-seat, thumb-in-mouth, yelling at siblings, whining and crying, and nagging or teasing. Kitchen timers can be used when a parent has been instructed to observe a given behavior for any specified interval from five minutes to an hour. This is especially useful if the monitor must observe for different periods of time or alternate periods of time. It is also useful when a child is expected to perform a given act, such as a chore, within so many minutes after he has been asked.

Premonitoring can be done using checklists like Vinter, Sarri, Vorwaller, and Schafer's (1966) Pupil Behavior Inventory. Although somewhat more subjective than counting because of the global nature of the responses, it is much easier

Table 2

GROUP SCORE CARD

BEHAVIOR		Sept 8	Sept 15	Sept 22	Sept 29	Oct 5	Oct 12	Oct 19	Oct 29
Assisting another boy (Each instance +1)	Pete								
	Alan								
	Fred								
	Gene								
	Harry								
Complimenting another boy (Each instance +1)	Pete								
	Alan								
	Fred								
	Gene								
	Harry								
Completing behavioral assignment (Each instance +2)	Pete								
	Alan								
	Fred								
	Gene								
	Harry								
Completing chore at meeting (Each instance +2)	Pete								
	Alan								
	Fred								
	Gene								
	Harry								
Teasing, bugging, breaking, tearing, hitting, shouting (Each instance −1)	Pete								
	Alan								
	Fred								
	Gene								
	Harry								
TOTAL									

to administer. Since considerable use of the instrument has been made, evidence of fairly high degree of reliability has been accumulated. However some therapists have found it too general even for a checklist and have developed their own. The following checklist can be used by having teachers either estimate frequencies (from frequently to never) or merely check those behaviors which are a problem. Once the checklist has been filled out, the therapist can determine which behaviors must be counted precisely.

1. *Gross motor*
   a. Getting out of seat
   b. Standing up
   c. Leaving room
   d. Turning around in seat
   e. Rocking
   f. Squirming
   g. Rocking
   h. Other
2. *Object noise*
   a. Tapping pencil or object
   b. Stamping feet, hands
   c. Desk or chair noises
   d. Other
3. *Disturbance of others' property*
   a. Grabbing objects
   b. Throwing objects
   c. In possession of another's property
   d. Destroying another's property
   e. Other
4. *Contact*
   a. Hitting
   b. Kicking
   c. Shoving
   d. Pinching
   e. Slapping
   f. Striking with object
   g. Other
5. *Verbalization*
   a. Talks without permission
   b. Makes irrelevant comments
   c. Swears
   d. Cries
   e. Talks with self
   f. Screams
   g. Tattles
   h. Tells others what to do
   i. Threatens others
   j. Teases
   k. Tells others what to do
   l. Name calls
   m. Lies
   n. Speaks in discussions
   o. Talks back
   p. Other
6. *Task behavior*
   a. Assignments completed
   b. Time on task
   c. Other
7. *Isolate behavior*
   a. Plays by self
   b. Participates in group activities
   c. Other
8. *Expressive behaviors*
   a. Sulks
   b. Has temper tantrums
   c. Has bad moods
   d. Maintains eye contact
   e. Smiles or laughs when reprimanded
   f. Other
9. *Other*
   a. Wets in pants
   b. Soils in pants
   c. Complains of illness
   d. Injures self
   e. Mouths object
   f. Absences
   g. Tardinesses
   h. Smells
   i. Other

Inventories similar to the one above have been developed for the home and for group meetings which often are briefer and more individualized. Checklists are best used as a means of identifying areas which need further specification but, because they are easily filled in and many parents and teachers dislike more exact procedures, checklists are all too often relied on as the sole source of data.

Charting

Regardless of the monitoring procedure used, the data must be recorded and summarized. To this end the therapist uses individual and group charts or graphs. The charts, when drawn to include the smallest improvement, often appear to be reinforcing in their own right and most children become enthusiastic over their accomplishments when they are presented visually. Figure 1 is a cumulative graph of the total number of homework assignments completed by group members.

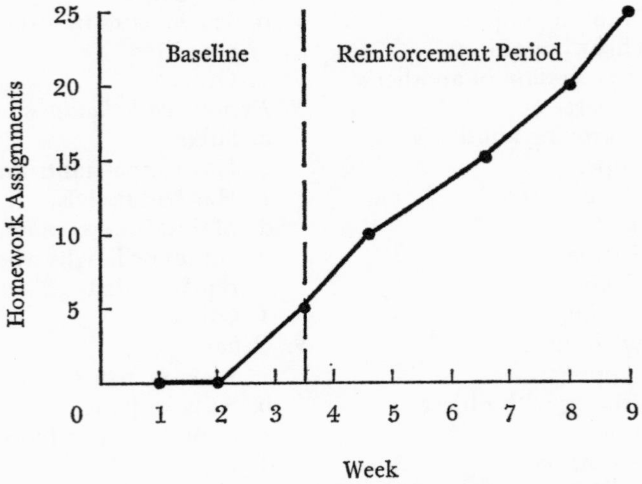

Figure 1 Group record of completed homework assignments.

The baseline and reinforcement period having been delineated, it is possible to see the effects of treatment. But not all graphs are cumulative. When trying to eliminate behaviors the therapist will often employ a noncumulative linear graph (see Figure 2). The graph illustrated in Figure 3 is cumulative and pictorial and is usually used for group goals. The goal in this case is the completion of seventy chores by all group members.

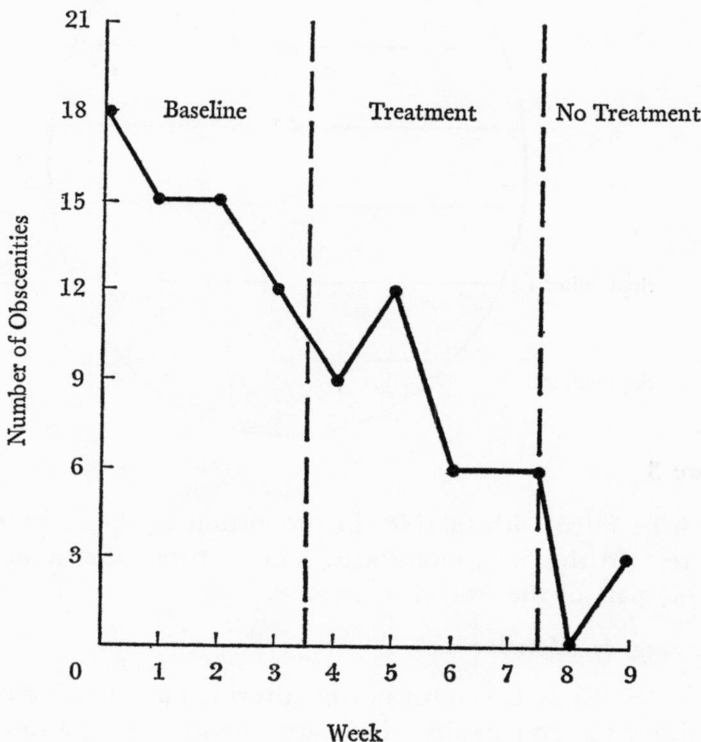

Figure 2 Number of obscenities uttered per meeting.

The group meeting room is often decorated with individual and group graphs and the first item of business is usually the collection and charting of the week's data. Therapists have often been creative in their use of colors or symbols. For example, one therapist used different lengths of crepe paper pasted on a wall to indicate group progress. Another, beginning with a shot glass, kept providing successively bigger glasses,

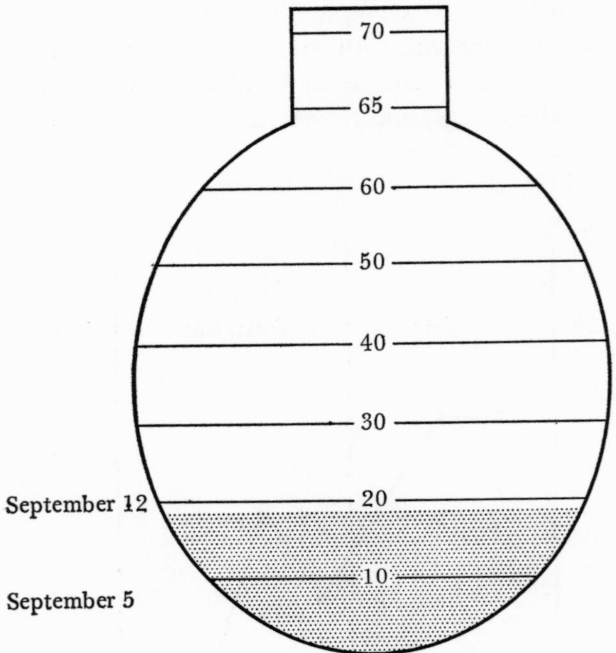

Figure 3

which he filled with marbles in proportion to the amount of progress. In this way, monitoring and charting become an enjoyable part of the treatment process.

Training to Monitor

Creativity is helpful but monitoring and charting often require skills and habits which are not in the repertoire of monitors other than the therapist. For this reason, when possible, monitors are trained in these skills. When an adult is being trained as a monitor, he is usually asked by the therapist to observe a discrete behavior of the therapist or other person present. Such clearly explicit behaviors as pulling a lock of hair or saying "you know" are tallied. The problems involved in this monitoring are then discussed and errors reviewed. The adult chooses a behavior he would like to observe at home or at school. The monitoring is usually checked out by the therapist after a few days to see whether there have been any problems. If it appears to be going well, more complex monitoring is recommended. If a stopwatch, timer, or counter is being used, the therapist demonstrates its use during the conference and encourages the adult to try it. If the parent or teacher is unable to learn the monitoring procedures (because of a lack of time or interest), community workers or group aides may be introduced as observers into the home or school. (The training of parents as monitors is discussed in more detail in Chapter Fifteen.)

Similar training methods are used for the child as monitor. However, the therapist may use the group meeting as the context of the training. Most group members view the training as a kind of game and participate willingly in "observation," first of the therapist, then of a relatively neutral behavior manifested by another in the group. Clients are then asked to observe a sibling doing something of little moral connotation or nuisance value, like the number of times a brother throws a baseball. The client later is required to watch the same sibling do something that annoys him or his parents. Still later he must count a behavior of his own as well as one of his peers.

Although carrying messages from teacher or parent to the group meeting is an important part of the monitoring process, many young children lack even this basic skill. Notes get crumpled, torn, and lost between the place of origin and destination. Reinforcement procedures are then used to shape up note-carrying behavior. The client may initially be reinforced simply for carrying a note. Later he may have to have it signed and bring it back. Finally, the note, now including information about the client, will have to be signed and delivered. Some clients are required to bring back evidence other than their own assertion to support a claim for completion of a behavioral assignment. They may show the therapist homework papers or bring a report card showing attendance. However, clients must first be trained to determine what evidence is and how one obtains it. A common error at this point is to assign untrained persons to monitor themselves or others. Should they fail, as they usually do, their interest in treatment often wanes. To prevent this, the therapist must be certain of the monitor's ability and motivation to make the necessary observations.

Once the client and/or significant others are trained in monitoring skills, the observable dimensions of both individual and group behavior can be determined. On the basis of baseline data, it is possible to estimate desirable levels of frequencies toward which individual members and the group as a whole can strive. How these goals are formulated and how the appropriate levels determined are discussed in the following chapter.

5

Goals and Plans for Treatment

Johnny agrees that he should learn the multiplication tables by next month. He will also increase his homework study time from one to one and a half hours per evening by next week.

Having just learned basketball skills, Argyle and Jerome will play basketball with each other two hours a week and stop playing with dolls in the school playroom.

All of the members of the group will increase their problem-oriented talk by at least one contribution per person per meeting and decrease their disruptive talk to a total of two disruptions by the end of the fourth meeting.

At the next meeting, the members will choose what group games they would like to participate in and will decide without the therapist's help how the games should be organized.

All of these are examples of goals—individual treatment goals, interactive treatment goals, group goals, and goals for a given meeting. Goals are statements of levels of behavior or arrangements of physical conditions to be achieved at some future time. In this chapter, I shall discuss each type of goal, how each is formulated, and how each relates to treatment planning. Let us look first at individual treatment goals, one or more of which is established with each individual member. These goals, which are derived from the initial description of the problem, involve a statement of expectations for relatively stable behavioral changes which will persist following treatment. Each goal is developed by the therapist with the client(s) on the basis of the following considerations.

Treatment Goals

Treatment goals, too, should be described in specific terms directly related to observable phenomena. They may point to abstract attitude or value changes only if the therapist specifies the observable indications of these changes. Otherwise, neither the therapist nor the client will know whether the treatment goals have been achieved. "Stronger self-esteem as indicated by fewer self-abusive statements, the obtaining and holding of a job, the finishing of his present night school course, attendance at social events . . ." is a general treatment goal defined in terms of observable indications of achievement.

Treatment goals should be formulated in terms of the client's behavior, attitudes, values, or expectations and *not* in terms of the therapist's activities. "Helping the client to find friends" is not a treatment goal, but the following statement is: "The client will approach other children, will learn to talk about subjects that interest them, and will learn to play those games that other neighborhood children his age play." Since "obtaining friends" may not be in the client's hands, thus is not included in the goal statement.

Treatment goals should be related to the client's expression of what it is he wants to change—especially if he is uncomfortable about his present behavior or circumstances—and should take into consideration his capacity for developing the skills necessary to achieve these goals. If motivation is high it is better to overestimate rather than underestimate his capacity. Early estimates of capacity may be misleading; after initial successes, the estimate of what the client can attain may be revised upward considerably. However, goals should also be related to endeavors for which at least occasional reinforcement may be available.

Consideration should also be given to the opportunities available to the client (his opportunity structure). Many clients cannot achieve their goals because money, certain types of schools, or certain societal positions are not available to them. It may be at least necessary to warn clients of this in borderline cases and to help them evaluate their goals in this light. Again, it is probably better to err on the side of optimism if client motivations are high. Some goals may be appropriate as personal goals but inappropriate as treatment goals, since they can not be facilitated by treatment. In other cases, the therapist may be involved or involve the client in an attempt to change his opportunity structure. Especially in minority groups, one does not lightly restrict an individual to his given opportunity structure, and the role of the therapist in this case is to clarify the risks and, once a decision is made, help the client facilitate goal attainment. It should also be remembered that treatment goals increase in value for the client if they are related to his long-range goals.

Treatment goals are limited by the procedures available to the therapist and allowed by the sponsoring agency. If the client has a medical problem, the therapist will help him find medical help, but the client will not have his medical cure as a treatment goal (although indeed a legitimate personal goal).

Frank, age eleven, referred to the treatment group because of his frequent swearing, has agreed to the goal of eliminating all obscenities directed toward teachers and the principal and using alternate expressions to show his dissatisfaction. Let us examine this goal in terms of the principles mentioned above. The goal is specific and certainly observable by teachers and the principal; it is a statement of Frank's verbal behavior. It is related to the general problem of classroom adjustment because almost every time the client uses obscene language toward the teacher he is expelled from class. The client has expressed a desire to remain in school since the alternative may be a training school. He has the capacity to control obscenities, evidenced by his restraint in the presence of his father (who beats Frank if he uses such language towards anyone at home). Success can result in praise by the therapist and teacher and negative reinforcement (the threat of being expelled is withdrawn). Elimination of the use of obscenities in class is a prerequisite for improving classroom performance since he has to be there to learn. By being reinforced for alternate expressions of his discontent and by being consistently removed for a two-minute period (time-out) for each profanity uttered, he can learn to eliminate obscenities. This is acceptable to the school and understandable to Frank. Since several members of the group have already learned this they can demonstrate it to Frank. Finally, it should be noted that the goal is not elimination of the use of obscenities in all situations. Frank has them under control at home but in his neighborhood the use of obscenities is part of the juvenile language.

Intermediate Treatment Goals

When treatment goals are too complex to attain in a short period of time, intermediate goals are established. Since the client's presenting problem includes a particular behavioral dimension occurring at intake (t_1) and the ultimate treatment goal involves assessment of the degree to which these same behaviors should be altered by the termination phase of treatment (t_3), the intermediate treatment goal refers to the same behavioral dimensions at a time (t_2) intermediate to intake and termination. This goal is established on the basis of what the therapist, in consultation with the client, assesses as attainable by the client between t_1 and t_2. The difference usually represents a change in intensity, frequency, or concomitant conditions in the behavioral areas of concern. It is, furthermore, an estimate of behavior as it should be within a short, overseeable, but meaningful time period. In this sense intermediate goals may be set at any time (which can be justified as a workable unit) between t_1 and t_3; that is, there usually should be a number of intermediate goals, each of which more nearly approximates the end goal (although not all the steps may be taken).

A client's intermediate treatment goals should be clearly related to his terminal goal, have specific and observable behavioral referents, and should be readily attainable once the previous intermediate goal has been reached. An example of an intermediate goal and its relation to presenting problem and terminal goal is presented below:

Presenting problem: Johnny, ten, "acts out"; that is, attacks other children in school, on the average of two times a week, so intensely that he and sometimes others are hurt in the process. It usually occurs when he is excessively fatigued or under pressure.

Terminal goal: Johnny's acting-out in school is eliminated, and Johnny controls this behavior without reminders from others.

Intermediate goal (possibility 1): Johnny's acting-out is reduced in intensity so there is no damage to Johnny or others.

Intermediate goal (possibility 2): Johnny's acting-out is reduced in frequency from several times a week to several times a month.

Intermediate goal (possibility 3): Johnny's acting-out is eliminated but the controls are external: reducing the pressure by limiting his work load and sending him home to sleep when he looks tired.

The chief advantage of intermediate goals is that they frequently point directly to the means of intervention which may be employed to bring about change. "Possibility 2" suggests isolation or "time-out from reinforcement" at the onset of acting-out behavior; "possibility 3" points directly to limiting work load and encouraging rest. Because "possibility 1" does not suggest any form of intervention, this possibility may be too general. Intermediate goals also provide a series of early and frequent successes in treatment when the long range treatment goal is so far in the distance that the client's lack of success would soon totally discourage him. A third advantage is that the process is highly explicit; the client knows where he started, what he should ultimately attain, and the steps he must take to get there. As Raven and Rietsma (1957) have demonstrated, knowledge of the pathway to the goal facilitates goal achievement. The process of setting intermediate goals is similar to the procedure of shaping. The former differs only insofar as it allows for unlimited intervention procedures, whereas shaping, in its pure form, primarily makes use of differential reinforcement.

Common and Group Treatment Goals

The therapist should help the members identify common and group treatment goals soon after treatment has begun. The setting and acceptance of operational goals for the group serve as a set of criteria by which its progress can be evaluated and a guide for group activity. The goals mobilize group skills and resources in a joint endeavor and when they are attained the group is reinforced to pursue more difficult tasks.

Common treatment goals are individual goals held in common by the members; for example, all the children in a group wish to improve their study behavior. Two individual goals related to this common goal are: the desire to increase studying behavior from zero to five hours per week; the desire to increase studying by increasing reading speed. In order to find commonality it is usually necessary to state individual treatment goals in rather general terms.

A common treatment goal differs from a group goal, which is the attainment of a desirable interactive pattern and the realization of some ultimate consequence. In some groups the interactive pattern is or becomes more important than the desired outcome. For example, a group of boys wants to be able to pass, shoot, and dribble the basketball better and to play more cooperatively than they do now so that they will win a basketball game. Or a group of girls wants to learn to play games without fighting with one another so that playing will be fun. Although the emphasis in the first example is on the outcome, in both examples future interactive patterns must be spelled out as part of the goal. If not such a group goal would have little value for the clinician or the group and would be, in the terms of Cartwright and Zander (1968, p. 409), a nonoperational group goal. Another type of group goal emphasizes the way in which a group should relate itself to its environment, other groups, the demands of the agency, or similar aspects of what Homans (1969) calls the external system. The group should become a part of the children's council at the settlement house. The group should raise money to send representatives to the next Boy Scout Jamboree. The group (in a juvenile group home) should assist one another to improve their personal appearances on visiting days.

As a group determines a long-range consequence for itself, the therapist must first encourage members to specify the appropriate interactive pattern and can then teach the behaviors of which the interactive pattern consists. Every group should have group goals, the attainment of which facilitates reaching individual goals. And, although it is not necessary for a group to have common treatment goals, communication among members may be drastically curtailed if individual problems are too diverse.

To facilitate the selection of group goals, the following interactive categories are suggested (see also Chapter Thirteen): (1) modification of the frequency of overt manifestation of affect among members; (2) modification of the affectional pattern (who likes/dislikes whom?) within the group; (3) establishment or modification of the pattern of distribution of work or the performance of group functions; (4) establishment or modification of the procedures by which the groups are governed or controlled; (5) increasing or decreasing general or specific intragroup interaction; (6) establishment or modification of procedures for planning group activities; (7) modification of a given group goal or procedure by which a group goal is selected; (8) carrying out of a given project and realization of its outcome.

Groups goals are characterized by different levels of difficulty and research concerning group aspirations has generated a number of hypotheses (Zander, 1968, pp. 118–216): (1)

Moderate increases in aspiration level generate comparable increases in performance. (2) Groups with goals of intermediate difficulty produce more than those with easier or more difficult goals. (3) Social pressures arising from outside the group can cause members to choose unreasonably high or unrealistically low group aspirations. Difficult goals seem to be more attractive than easy goals. (4) When a group succeeds it raises its level of aspiration; when the group fails, it lowers the level. The raising tendency seems much stronger and more consistent than the lowering one.

The implication for the group therapist is that group goals should be of moderate difficulty (considering the skills of the group and time allotted for attainment) and that if the group, by virtue of social pressures, chooses goals with a high probability of failure, the therapist should either encourage the setting of less difficult subgoals or should train the members in the skills they need to attain the desired goals. If subgoals are set, they should not be so difficult that they cannot be attained in the designated time period. Not all goals require successive approximations. But the therapist should carefully evaluate whether the skills and resources required for goal attainment are available to the group before he adds his support to a goal pronouncement. A group may choose what the therapist considers an inappropriate goal without his overt concurrence, however, and this is usually worth the risk of failure in terms of the commitment involved in setting goals in the face of the therapist's advice. As Zander (1968) also points out, "The more members are committed to a group or feel responsible for its fate, the more they develop a desire for group achievement of success."

Objectives for Group Meetings

Group goals may be established for any point in the group's interactive history. The group may decide to accomplish one or a few goals by the end of a given set of meetings or not until the end of treatment. In order to structure his preparation, therefore, the therapist should formulate objectives for every meeting and/or short series of meetings. These objectives may include changes in the interactive pattern of the group, changes in other group characteristics, and changes in individual behavior in the direction of the given individual treatment goal. The first two objectives, if agreed upon by group members, are short term group goals. The last objective is a short term individual treatment goal. Examples of goals for a meeting are the following: reduction of intragroup competition (change in interactive pattern of the group); increasing attractiveness of the group (change in group characteristics); and increasing frequency of Don's participation in the group (changes in individual behavior).

The therapist's objectives for meetings, like all goals, must be formulated in terms of observable events. Moreover, each objective should be followed by a rationale which is formulated in terms of ultimate consequences and its contribution to the attainment of long range goals.

Each of these objectives and its respective rationale should be followed by a treatment plan. If the objectives do not suggest one, they are usually improperly formulated. If the group has already chosen its program activities, the therapist should determine in what way these activities can be used in the service of attaining any meaningful objectives which are compatible with the program. And if situations occur which will facilitate long range treatment goals or group goal attainment, the therapist should be flexible enough to work them into the meeting. Although the therapist formulates meeting objectives, they must be compatible with the members' interests. Many therapists, therefore, formulate final plans with the group members or a representative delegation, or present them to the group for discussion.

Treatment Plans

Once goals have been formulated, treatment plans can be developed, which is simply a description of procedures to be used for amelioration of the presenting problems. More specifically, a treatment plan consists of a brief description of the problems and goals, the monitoring procedures and charts to be used, alternate treatment procedures and their rationale, and eventually the design for stabilization and transfer of change. A group plan consists of the above information as it applies to common problems and the alteration of various group attributes. It also contains details as to when, where, and how often the group meets, the nature of auxiliary contacts, the types of group tasks and group reinforcement, and procedures for delegating treatment responsibility to group members.

Plans, of course, are not static. As information accrues through the monitoring system they must be evaluated in terms of their ongoing effectiveness and often the procedures and goals will need revision; sometimes totally new plans are required. Initial plans are meant as a sort of procedural outline and should assume a more definitive form as treatment progresses.

The following example of a treatment plan has been provided by a therapist in a school setting. Individual treatment goals and charts have been omitted for the sake of brevity.

Presenting problem: A third grade teacher was upset by the high frequency of fighting, name-calling, and stealing she observed among seven of her boys. She was also concerned that their behavior might spread to others in the class whom they strongly influenced.

Common goals: Decrease frequency of hitting, stealing, fighting, name-calling, and lying; increase frequency of peer-helping; increase keeping-out-of-trouble behavior; increase mutually reinforcing verbal behavior.

Initial group goals: Increasing attractiveness of the group, integrating two boys into the group's communication pattern who have adjusted to the demands of the classroom, and establishing norm of treatment focus in the group.

Monitoring: Teacher willing to count incidents of behaviors mentioned above and to report these daily to the therapist, who would keep a group chart.

Group composition: In addition to the boys with problems, two others will be added to the group who have no problems but whom the teacher has indicated are very good at helping others.

Preliminary group plan: Therapist will meet weekly with

the group for forty-five minutes. After six weeks, outcome will be evaluated with the teacher and boys to see whether the group should be continued. Meetings will be divided into two parts—problem talk and activities. Refreshments will be given at the first few meetings "just for coming"; later these will be contingent on the performance of behavioral assignments. Individual and group charts will be displayed in the meeting room. Paper money for group trips and group surprises can be earned for participation in problem talk and role plays. Person with most money chooses the games to be played during activities. Individual assignments to be performed in the classroom will be given to each member on the basis of his most serious problem. Paper money can be earned for their completion. Role plays will be used to demonstrate how to avoid fights and to provide practice in avoidance.

In this example the reader should note that after presentation of the problems involved, both common and initial group goals were established. On the basis of these the therapist was able to make plans for monitoring, group composition, and preliminary treatment procedures. Neither the goals nor the change procedures is static. As new information accumulates each is subject to evaluation and change. Before the therapist can devise a treatment plan, he must know what procedures are available to him for achieving the goals mentioned above. Contingency management, contracts and assignments, modeling and rehearsal procedures, and desensitization are central procedures in most individual and group plans and are discussed in the following chapters.

6

Increasing Adaptive Behavior

After the meeting the four boys swept the room, put away the toys, and replaced the benches and table in the center of the room. For each chore completed satisfactorily, the therapist praised the boy warmly and put a check on the group chart. Twenty checks would earn a trip to the zoo.

Roger, Lucky, and Zelmo were discussing what got them in trouble with the police. After each five minutes of discussion the kitchen timer would go off, at which point the therapist distributed tokens to each child who had participated in the discussion during that period. Tokens could be used to purchase slot cars.

For every five arithmetic problems each boy in the group completed, he received a small candy.

In each of these examples the therapist or group members responded to a given set of behaviors by one or more group members with praise, material goods, food, or tokens. In each example the consequences were administered on the basis of some prior agreement. The relationship of behavior to consequences is referred to as the response-reinforcement contingency, which can also be described as an "if . . . then . . ." statement: *If* such behavior occurs *then* such a consequence will follow. In the above examples all contingencies have been arranged by the therapist or the group. But even if there had been no prearrangements, consequences would still have ensued. As Homme and Tosti (1965, p. 16) point out, "Either one manages the contingencies or they get managed by accident. Either way there will be contingencies and they will have their effect."

Social Reinforcement

Of the available types of reinforcement, human response appears to be the most potent reinforcer of social behavior. The use of praise, a wink, a touch, a movement in the direction of the subject, a smile, a criticism are major influences on our daily behavior. Even the use of material reinforcement is enhanced when issued by a person attractive to the subject. Although most social reinforcement is given uncontingently in traditional therapies, the client must earn social reinforcement in behavioral treatment. The therapist compliments the child for accomplishments specified in advance as desirable and is careful, moreover, not to satiate the child with praise or nonverbal indications of approval (especially in regard to accomplishments other than those the child is working on at the moment).

Of course, effective social reinforcement is dependent on each individual's reinforcement history. Although attention is reinforcing for most children, only adult attention and in the form of screaming, is effective for others; some seek only peer attention, and for others any attention, no matter what its nature or from whom it originates, is reinforcing. Assessment, of course, must take into consideration the effect of individual reinforcement on the group and vice versa. The indiscriminate application of social reinforcement in the group is probably less disruptive of group interaction than the indiscriminate use of aversive stimuli, but both may result in unpredictable behavior change.

One form of social reinforcement in particular that appears to have a strong influence on the behavior of group members is social evaluation. Many therapies are based solely on the use of negative evaluations of behavior as an impetus to change. In a behavioral approach group evaluations of individual achievement are encouraged in group discussion, and peer approval is harnessed in service of prosocial goals. This is not to deny, however, the importance of social criticism when combined with social reinforcement which will be discussed in greater detail further on.

One of the major advantages of the group as the context of treatment is the opportunity to provide the members with the large number of reinforcing activities usually unavailable to the isolated child in treatment. Even such individualized activities as model-making appear to be more reinforcing when others are present. Except for the withdrawn or socially overexposed child, most clients value interactive over isolated activities. As a result, social interactive activities or group tasks comprise one of the major reinforcement procedures in group treatment. Tasks also provide the discriminative stimulus or structure which facilitates certain types of desirable behaviors. Specific use of group activities or tasks as reinforcement and discriminative stimuli is discussed extensively in Chapter Eleven.

Of course not all interactive activities are desirable or prosocial. Children may enjoy running around the classroom screaming at the top of their lungs and may prefer unorganized horseplay to organized studying. However, as Premack (1959) has observed, high probability behavior may be used as a reinforcer for low probability behavior. Children may be reinforced for sitting quietly in their seats for five minutes with equal time for running around the room. In a group of shy children, participation in five minutes of discussion was rewarded by fifteen minutes of isolated activities. In a group of highly aggressive children, the same amount of group discussion was rewarded by five minutes of wild horseplay. In all of these cases the allotted frequency for undesirable behavior was gradually reduced as the demand for the desirable behavior was increased.

For most children contingently applied social reinforcement is sufficient to maintain desirable behaviors and teach new ones. However, for those children whose maladaptive behaviors are well learned, whose reinforcement repertoire is limited, and for whom the usual social reinforcement is ineffective, more concrete reinforcement is required. Most children in treatment fall into one of these categories.

Token and Material Reinforcement

Social reinforcement, either verbal or nonverbal, is seldom isolated from material reinforcement. Since many clients come from either socially or materially deprived backgrounds or both, material goods are powerful reinforcers, especially early in treatment. Praise and various nonverbal indications of interest or affection often represent ambiguous cues at best and at worst are indications that someone is going to deprive them of something. For such children material rewards are dispensed initially but are paired with praise and nonverbal encouragement in order to establish the latter as social reinforcement. One of the problems of material reinforcement is that highly valued objects may be too large to administer every time a person performs a desirable act and it is for this reason that tokens are often used. Tokens, like pennies, have a small value and can be used, when a sufficient number have been accumulated, to purchase desirable material goods or social activities. "Tokens" may be poker chips, painted blocks, play money, clicks on a counter, tally marks on a tabulation sheet, pennies, stars, or any other visible indicator of achievement. The tokens are later paired (by a system of exchange) with desirable objects (see below) or with activities.

Tokens, aside from their size, are highly manipulable, their value can be varied, and they are observable; the child always knows that he and his peers are getting something when they receive a token which is not always the case with praise (see Thomas, 1967). Tokens are given immediately following conformity to group rules, completion of individual behavioral assignments, and performance of any spontaneous behaviors whose frequency the therapist wishes to increase. They also may be given following a predetermined time period when at least one or more desirable acts are performed or when a stated number of undesirable acts are not performed.

Tokens can be used to make purchases from a "store" of items displayed before the group. Differing in value, the objects can include candy bars, model airplanes, cosmetics, tickets to professional sports events, tickets to a beauty show, tickets for a trip with the worker, and credits for purchases at a local snack bar. In addition, some therapists have developed catalogs from which objects can be purchased at a later date. If a point or star system is not used, each member keeps his own tokens during the course of the meeting and turns in to the therapist those tokens he does not spend. The therapist keeps them in an envelope until the next meeting to prevent trading or other manipulation of chips outside the group. It is important that great care be taken in the bookkeeping because tokens are so important to most members that even minor errors may result in emotional outbursts or disruptive behaviors. In those groups in which saving is encouraged, many highly priced items may be placed in the store; conversely, if hoarding is a problem behavior or if the group needs more immediate and frequent gratification, the therapist can require that half the tokens earned in a given meeting must be spent at the end of that meeting.

There is considerable variation in the price of given items or events and how many tokens different activities earn. These decisions depend to a large degree on the value placed on items by the children, but the therapist may also use low cost to facilitate purchase of items in which he would like members to develop an interest. For example, in the menu below models cost anywhere from twenty to 150 tokens, but a dictionary cost only twelve.

The group of twelve to thirteen year olds for whom this menu was developed was especially interested in model building; the bubble gum and candy bars were included for low earners and children who required reinforcement at short intervals.

STORE ITEMS

Item	*Cost in Tokens*
Drag Coupe	150
Sport Coupe	80
1932 Ford	50
Cleveland Cruiser	40
Air Lines Proctor, Air Lines Supermarine	25
Wooden Glider	18
Dictionary	12
All Candy Bars	10
Glue	5
Bubble Gum	3

Most groups remain in the token economy only in the initial phase of treatment, which may be extended for younger groups. As behaviors become reinforced by persons in extragroup situations or as the behaviors become self reinforcing, tokens are removed first from one and later several activities. The announcement that tokens have been removed altogether usually provokes renewed discussion of the reasons for being in the group and of the ultimate goal of changing behavior without the aid of tangible reinforcement.

Group Reinforcement

In order to make use of the reinforcement value which peers have for each other in group treatment, contingencies are often designed for the entire group (Wodarski and others, 1971). Group contingencies engender a great deal of pressure on each member to perform what is expected of him in order that everyone obtain the reward. If the group is valued by the individual, the pressure is a highly effective device for behavioral change. However, if the individual has more attractive alternatives, the pressure may be ignored or he may even leave the group.

The greatest pressure is achieved by making the group reinforcement dependent on the behavior of one person. The therapist must be certain, in such cases, that the individual is capable of performing the assigned task and that the only reason for failure will be his decision not to cooperate. Even so, such high-pressure situations should be undertaken with care. Group contingencies are sometimes inadvisable in the initial treatment phases when the attractiveness of the group is low, because the group's influence will be low also. Nor are group contingencies recommended when one member has a consistent pattern of punishing group members. He may be reinforced by the negative attention his noncooperation stimulates.

With these qualifications it appears that group contingencies are a necessary adjunct to all other treatment tools utilized by the group therapist. There is extensive research to support the assumption that behaviors can be maintained more readily with group rather than individual contingencies (Wodarski and others, 1971; Lovitt, Guppy, and Blatner, 1969; Hamblin, Buckholdt, Ferritor, Kozlof, and Blackwell, 1971). Moreover, group contingencies facilitate group development and provide the members with equal amounts of reinforcement.

A variation, which combines individual with group contingencies, is to present tokens to each member for his particular desirable performance. The tokens are counted at the end of the meeting and an equivalent number of tokens are added to the group total. In addition each client can use his own tokens to make purchases in the "store" or can save them for later purchase of larger items. This procedure can be used early in treatment as a means of maintaining individual accomplishment in the face of group failure. However, this variation reduces group pressure on the deviant. A similar approach, combining individual praise and group contingency, was used effectively to increase the popularity of junior high school students (Alden, Pettigrew, and Skiba, 1970).

Another type of group reinforcement can be carried out with a tape recorder or 8 mm. camera. Group behavior is filmed or taped provided certain standards are being met (cooperative behavior is manifested, there is no loud talking, swearing, or fighting). As soon as undesirable behaviors appear the tape (camera) is turned off, bell is rung, the timer is set for five minutes, and the recorder or cameraman sits down. When the timer rings, taping is begun again. This is a group time-out-from-reinforcement procedure which also can be effectively used in the classroom. Variations are also possible: the interval between stopping and beginning the tape can be extended or varied as one attempts to stabilize the new group norms, and group members can earn points for the group to buy minutes of listening or viewing time. (Compare with Meyer, Strowig, and Hosford, 1970.)

In order to facilitate the selection and use of group contingencies, a number of group activities and other rewards that I have found effective are suggested here. Since most adolescents do not have access to automobiles, riding in a car chauffeured by the therapist through the members' home areas has been highly attractive and has simultaneously increased the status of the treatment group in the community. The purchase of a junkyard car has been an attractive reward for older boys. Moreover, the group can earn time to work on it, and if it eventually runs, to learn to drive it. Group sports (swimming, basketball, ice-skating, sailing, horseback-riding, bowling) are also rewarding, but only if the children have minimal skills for participation. Before these sports can be used on a contingency basis the therapist may first have to stimulate interest in them with models, films, books, and an initial experience. Once the group is interested, the commitment to work to earn these rewards has been impressive. If they can be stimulated and minimal skills learned, activities such as horseback-riding, camping, and sailing are particularly useful with juvenile offenders who are unable to obtain these experiences through their delinquent activities.

A visit by or to sports stars, disc-jockeys, or civil rights organizers is also a frequently used reward for both boys and girls; it is especially valued if the star gives lessons in his area of expertise. He or she can also serve as a role model for the group members. Beauty parlor appointments at a local beautician college have been a potent reward for girls. Dancing lessons and lessons in make-up and personal appearance, first used noncontingently, also become effective rewards. Restaurant meals are attractive to both boys and girls, although the necessary restaurant behaviors may have to be shaped, modeled, and rehearsed. After one successful experience, this becomes a highly valued reward.

Expanding Reinforcement Repertoires

Clients often have only limited interests, and these may be delinquent or otherwise maladaptive. In order to broaden the reinforcing effectiveness of the therapist it is necessary to present clients, uncontingently, with the possibility of participating in a large number of events. This procedure is called reinforcement sampling (Ayllon and Azrin, 1968b). These events, such as the make-up lessons or restaurant meals, are paired with existing reinforcers such as riding in an automobile, in order to condition the new events as secondary reinforcers. Once these events are chosen freely by the clients, they can be considered primary reinforcers and must be earned.

In addition to reinforcement sampling, modeling procedures are also used to increase the clients' reinforcement repertoires. If the model (older children, celebrities) attends a group meeting, he is asked to participate in activities which up to that moment have not been regarded as attractive by the members. The model not only serves as reinforcement but as a means of enhancing the reinforcement repertoire of the clients.

Shaping New Behavior

Even when ample reinforcement exists, a common error in its application is the attempt to reinforce a behavior that is totally absent from an individual's repertoire. A behavior must appear at least once in order to be reinforced. For this reason a number of procedures are used to obtain an initial performance of the behavior. Occasionally it is sufficient to tell a person what he should do; when he does it he is reinforced. When the problem is more complex, a demonstration by a model may evoke the behavior (see Chapter Nine). The most common procedure is the use of shaping; that is, reinforcement of successive approximations of the desired end behavior.

Although prior to treatment Alan did talk in two-person groups or with members of his family, he had not previously spoken in larger social situations. Alan not only did not speak in his classroom, he did not look at others while they were talking to him. In order to shape his verbal participation, the therapist first reinforced Alan's occasional (perhaps accidental) eye contact with whomever was speaking. The reinforcers were a token, praise, a smile, and sometimes a wink. When brief eye contact increased in frequency, the therapist and two older boys who were working with the group as models reinforced only prolonged eye contact (five seconds or more). After Alan began to look regularly for prolonged periods at those around him, he was reinforced only for eye contact and some physical indication that he was listening (a nod or a word). Since such physical indications did not increase at once, the therapist also prompted him to nod or grunt at times. When it was clear he was listening, he was reinforced only for verbal responses of one or more words and, finally, phrases or complete sentences were required before he received reinforcement.

Pure shaping is seldom carried out (for an example, however, see Skinner, 1953) since prompting, instructional and modeling procedures are often included. Shaping is difficult within the context of the group because of the bootleg (unplanned for) reinforcement which group members often provide each other for approximations of a desired behavior which are no longer being reinforced or even for maladaptive behaviors which are incompatible with the behavior being shaped. In order to limit this reinforcement, group members are often involved in planning the shaping paradigm or providing the reinforcement.

Juvenile offenders whose major habitat is the street corner of an inner city are not likely to speak readily or openly to a psychologist or street worker. In order to develop effective participation in behavioral therapy for these adolescents, Schwitzgebel and Kolb (1964) used shaping. First the authors rented a storefront in the neighborhood and after the boys were accustomed to seeing them around, they let it be known that in the service of their research they would pay the boys for short periods of time spent in dictating their street experiences into a tape recorder. They could stop in any time they wished. After the word got around, boys began to trickle in; they were greeted warmly and given refreshments as well as a salary for their brief and unstructured efforts. As the boys became more comfortable with the tape recorder, the authors gradually imposed restrictions. Appointments had to be made; then they had to be on time. Gradually, the tape recorder was faded out as the object to which they talked, and the therapist was faded in. Finally the boys were talking comfortably to a therapist, who helped them find ways of developing skills in manual arts and electronics, which the boys thought they needed.

Teaching Behavioral Chains

Many of the behaviors dealt with in group treatment consist of series of related events or chains of responses. These responses are linked by small, often implicit, reinforcing events and by discriminative stimuli provided by the proceeding response. For example, the child who is learning to study must sit in the chair at his desk; take out a pencil, piece of paper, and a book; read a paragraph; take notes on what he reads; and so forth. One can either reinforce him only at the end of this process, which might result in reinforcing only the last action performed, or one can reinforce each step (starting with the last) and as each is mastered reinforce the previous step in order to teach the whole chain. As the response is learned, the reinforcement is eliminated and discrete responses begin to operate as smooth chains. The assumption is that the overt reinforcer eventually becomes an implicit reinforcing stimulus, and the previous event becomes the discriminative stimulus for the next event (see Staats and Staats, 1963).

The advantage of viewing complex behavior as a chain is that it provides a system for breaking these behaviors into smaller temporal parts which are sufficiently concise to be readily observed and reinforced when they occur. Moreover, it provides increased opportunities for success and a high level of reinforcement.

Schedules of Reinforcement

Thus far reinforcement usually has been discussed as if it always follows every presentation of a given behavior. Although this juxtaposition of behavior and consequence does occur or can be made to occur, many other arrangements also exist, each presenting a unique contribution to the modification or stabilization of behavior. Ferster and Skinner (1957) provide an extensive description of the effects of various arrangements on the speed and acquisition of a response, the strength at which it is maintained, and the decrease of an established response. Only some of these will be reviewed here.

Group treatment initially attempts immediate reinforcement of most desirable behaviors whenever they occur (continuous reinforcement). Perfect continuity is not possible since the reinforcing agents often do not see the given behavior every time it occurs. Some behaviors (task completion, for example) can be reinforced more effectively on the basis of their occurrence during a given time period of time (fixed interval reinforcement). Therapists often reinforce high frequency behaviors after a given number of performances of the behavior (fixed ratio reinforcement). Reinforcement for successive performances of a given behavior may be given after an irregular number of occurrences of the behavior (variable ratio reinforcement). For example, Pete was issued a token after four observed instances of eye contact, a second token after two instances of eye contact, and a third token after eight instances of eye contact. Group members may also be reinforced at intervals of varying lengths (variable interval reinforcement). The most common reinforcement schedules in daily life are a combination of variable interval and variable ratio.

In the initial phase of treatment, reinforcement is distributed according to schedules which most nearly approximate continuous or small fixed ratios and intervals. There is strong evidence to support the notion that this is the quickest way to build up the frequency of a behavior in the repertoire of an organism (Ferster and Skinner, 1957). When the behavior is occurring at acceptable frequencies or appropriate intervals, the frequency of reinforcement is gradually reduced by increasing the length of the interval or the size of the ratio. Eventually the intervals and ratios become variable, and intermittent mixed schedules often become the rule. This process is referred to as "thinning the reinforcement schedule." Thinning is used as a means of increasing the behaviors' resistance to extinction. Although behaviors build up more quickly under a rich reinforcement schedule, they tend to be quickly extinguished if reinforcement is terminated (Ferster and Skinner, 1957). Although highly sophisticated adjustments of reinforcement schedules have been developed, only rough schedule alterations tend to be used in the group situation because of the problems involved in treating many behaviors and many people at the same time. However, there has been growing care and technical skill invested in the planned application of reinforcement schedules.

As I pointed out earlier, continuous reinforcement is difficult because of the limited observation capacity of one therapist. The use of observers or group members as monitors and even as agents of reinforcement tends to reduce this problem, as does definition of the behavior in highly discrete and specific terms. However, variables such as task completion are easier to observe and reward than task-oriented talk, and sometimes the crucial behavior may not lend itself to explicit definition. For the same reason fixed ratios are even more difficult to administer than continuous ones. Even with the use of a hand counter, it is difficult to watch the counter and lead the group at the same time. Fixed or even variable intervals are more readily carried out because the bell of the timer abruptly reminds the therapist when the period is finished. The major problem of variable or intermittent schedules is that reinforcement is often thinned too rapidly, resulting in extinction of the desired behavior.

As the reader has seen in this chapter, the therapist expends a great deal of effort in teaching new behaviors or in increasing the frequency of behaviors already in the repertoires of his group members. He is constantly reinforcing or training others to reinforce, is shaping, increasing reinforcement repertoires, and adjusting reinforcement schedules. But at times he must also help decrease the frequency of some behaviors or even eliminate them. In the next chapter procedures for attaining this end are described.

7

Decreasing Maladaptive Behaviors

For every ten minutes that Ida played with other group members without hitting them, she received a token.

When Alan complained or tried to tease the other boys, they all agreed to ignore him.

Any child who initiated a fight or climbed on the fire escape was removed for two minutes from the game room and placed in the small office next door.

When Margaret tore up Eileen's painting the group members fined her five cents, just as they had done when Anita broke the pencil sharpener and Ann wrote on the desk with her pen.

There are some behaviors which must be reduced in frequency or even eliminated if the client is to be able to cope effectively with his environment. The group procedures utilized in this instance include positive reinforcement of other behaviors than the maladaptive behavior; positive reinforcement for the non-emission of the behavior under conditions which usually evoke it; extinction; time-out from reinforcement; response cost; and aversive stimuli or punishment. Although a few forms of aversive stimulation are used in group treatment, positive reinforcement procedures are usually preferred in order to reduce the possibility that the therapist will become associated with the aversive stimuli or that the client will avoid the stimuli by dropping treatment prematurely.

Reinforcement of Other Behavior

Reinforcement can be used in two ways to reduce the frequency of undesirable behavior. The first is differential reinforcement of all behaviors other than the maladaptive one. For example, in a group of shy, withdrawn children, crying in response to criticism or other pressures was one behavior the therapist and clients agreed to decrease in frequency. Under the conditions of criticism or other social pressure, if a child responded in any way other than to cry he was reinforced by a token and the praise of the therapist.

The second procedure gives reinforcement if the undesired behavior does not occur during a specified period of time. The timer is set for the given time, and if it rings prior to the performance of the undesired behavior, a reinforcer is distributed. If the undesired behavior does occur, nothing happens when the timer goes off. Although it is usually more effective to reinforce specific alternative behaviors, the latter procedure is useful in the early phases of treatment when the alternatives have not yet been identified. It can be effectively used in groups, either for nonoccurrence of a common behavior, such as yelling, or for individual behaviors over a common period of time. For example, if Alice is working on yelling, Eugenia on fighting, and Tanya on pouting, each would receive a token when the timer rang, provided she had not displayed her specific undesirable behavior.

Extinction

Extinction is the process of weakening a response by nonreinforcement. Numerous examples of the use of this technique with children have been cited in the literature. Temper tantrums, in particular, have responded to this treatment procedure (Williams, 1959; Carlson, 1968; Holder, 1969). However, a wide range of other behaviors have also succumbed to extinction procedures. Since much maladaptive behavior seems to be maintained by the attention it receives, the withholding of attention appears to be the significant factor in treatment.

In some cases maladaptive behaviors increase in frequency following the introduction of extinction procedures. And before the behavior weakens, a number of side effects may be noted: aggression toward the previous reinforcer of the maladaptive behavior; random aggressiveness toward individuals or objects in the vicinity; and crying, whining, or moping. If attention in some form is given during this period, these emotional effects are reinforced. This is probably the way in which most forms of maladaptive emotional and physical responses to frustrating situations are shaped in the first place. It is imperative, therefore, that the extinction procedure be maintained and especially in the face of emotional side effects. Some side effects of extinction may be disruptive to the group and in this case other measures may be taken, the most powerful of which is the time-out procedure. The therapist may also cue the client that the time-out procedure is about to occur or that various forms of mild punishment may be used. In general the extinction procedure is preferable because the disruptive side effects of punishment are usually much stronger. Moreover, many clients are so accustomed to punishment that it is no longer an effective control procedure.

Extinction procedures in a group are complicated by the fact that not only must the therapist extinguish behavior but the entire group must be trained to extinguish it as well. The most frequent misuse of extinction in a group is for the therapist to ignore behavior (withhold attention) while the members laugh or fight with the individual who is manifesting the maladaptive behavior. For example, Tom, age eleven, clowned in all social situations. The therapist chose to extinguish the clowning by ignoring it. The other members, however, roared with laughter when Tom put on the therapist's coat backward, climbed in and out the window, and ran around the meeting room. After considering his failure the therapist changed the procedure by training the other members not to respond. Every time they imitated the therapist (he gave a cue) in ignoring Tom's behavior, they each received a token. In this way Tom received reinforcement from neither the therapist nor the other group members for clowning.

While the extinction plan is in operation, reinforcement should be presented following adaptive behaviors or even following a given time period in which the maladaptive behavior is absent. If maladaptive behaviors are his prime source for attention, the child will need alternative successful sources if extinction is to work effectively. Williams (1959) advised parents to give a child considerable attention before putting him to bed, to read him stories, and then to leave and give no attention to ensuing temper tantrums.

Time-Out From Reinforcement

One of the most frequent procedures used to control disruptive social behaviors is time-out from reinforcement. The child is removed from all reinforcing stimuli for a brief period of time to control such behaviors as temper tantrums, swearing, silliness, teasing, and fighting. A time-out usually lasts from thirty seconds to five minutes in a quiet place where reinforcers are limited. To be effective, the use of time-out presupposes that the person is under fairly high reward conditions. The time-out is usually given immediately following the undesirable behavior in a direct, matter of fact, assertive tone of voice. For example when a child initiates a fight he is told immediately and firmly, "The rule is that we do not fight in the meeting room. Now you must go to the time-out room. As soon as you are quiet, I shall count one minute and let you know when you can return." The child may at first need to be escorted to the time-out location; if he refuses to go, complains, or cries, all activity stops until he leaves and quiets down. When the time-out period is up, the therapist goes to the child and says matter of factly that he may return to the activity room. On the rare occasion that the child says he does not wish to return, the therapist leaves him in the time-out room until he changes his mind.

Patterson and White (1969, p. 3), on the basis of their survey of experiments and clinical reports of time-out, come to the following conclusions: (As quoted by Kanfer and Phillips, 1970, p. 362).

> (1) In a variety of situations, especially the classroom, TO [time-out] has been more efficient and effective than what might be termed "passive ignoring." (2) Although TO of long duration has been used . . . short periods have the added advantage of allowing for an increase in the time available for positive reinforcement of acts representative of social skills. (3) Size of TO rooms needn't be restricted to cramped quarters. Studies reporting effective use of TO have used rooms about the size of a small bedroom. (4) Maintaining supervision of TO while in use is desirable. It is necessary in studies where the child is to be returned to class immediately following cessation of tantrum behavior. . . . In addition, several investigators subscribe to the notion that high amplitude destructive or verbal behavior in TO should be mildly punished by telling the child that, "That cost you two more minutes. Every time you kick the door, it is two more minutes." There are, however, no data which demonstrate the outcome of this procedure. (5) TO procedures avoid some of the problems associated with the use of direct physically painful punishment. . . . For example, use of TO, contrasted with physically aggressive punishment methods, does not provide the child with an aggressive model for imitation . . . that is, no models displaying methods of counter aggression which could be used against parents, teachers, or peers.

Although time-out usually is used with younger children, Tyler and Brown (1967) describe an experiment in the use of time-out in the form of brief, swift isolation as a means of controlling behavior of adolescent residents of a training school cottage while in the recreation room. Whenever a resident broke the rules, he was immediately put into his room for a short period of time. The study was divided into four phases: during the first and third phases confinement was used, and in the second and fourth reprimands were given. The time-out confinement was much more effective. Time-out from reinforcement is more difficult in group than in family or institutional treatment unless the group is highly attractive. If this is so, however, it can be used with excellent results. One therapist contracted with the group to use time-out whenever one group member began to tease someone. When the teasing occurred the therapist at once indicated time-out, and the offender was immediately sent to the next room for one minute. If he did not go, all action stopped. As a result, the pressure was so great on most offenders that they were unwilling to sabotage the group by refusing to go.

Response Costs

Response cost is the removal of a positively reinforcing stimulus from the environment following a behavioral response (Weiner, 1962). In a token economy, then, certain behaviors, such as the uttering of obscenities, result in fines. There is always the danger, however, that treatment will degenerate into a strictly response cost program since it seems easier to identify unadaptive than adaptive behavior. For this reason, as a rule of thumb, therapists are instructed to keep the proportion of tokens issued to tokens taken away at an arbitrary ratio of four to one. The therapist then remains a reinforcing stimuli rather than an agent of punishment.

Response cost in group treatment can also be used to reduce free time or gym time, or to cancel such activities as trips and attendance at athletic events. Unless carried out contractually, this approach tends to be used too arbitrarily; that is, when the mood of the therapist rather than the behavior of the clients warrants it. However, when it is stated that the group trip is contingent on certain sets of behavior, withdrawing the right to the trip for defined disruptive behaviors appears to be an effective control procedure. Temporary removal of group activities has an additional disadvantage in that a set of stimulus conditions has been removed also which might have provided a rich training situation. For example, a child who needed to learn to play with children lost his recess (along with his classmates) and was unable to try out a newly-learned skill.

Staff administration of heavy response costs does not appear to be as effective with adolescents as the administration of lighter costs by a representative of the group. In a study evaluating the effectiveness of a token system for predelinquent boys, Phillips (1968) discovered that large token penalities given to the entire group failed to reduce their maladaptive behaviors. On the other hand the same behaviors were quickly eliminated when a group member, in his role as manager, levied lesser fines. (For a further discussion of response cost see Kanfer and Phillips 1970, pp. 362–364.)

Punishment

The presentation of aversive stimuli or punishment is seldom used as an explicit procedure in group treatment. One common practice, however, in the face of persistent deviant behavior, is confrontation of the deviant by peer reaction. Confrontation has been used often by therapists of various orientations without the acknowledgment that it is a punishment procedure. In spite of emotional side effects, the technique seems useful.

Lou teased Terry with little or no response. Then he began to work on Ted, who told him to "shut up." Finally Lou began to needle Pete, who turned around and took a swing at Lou. At this point the therapist interceded and asked the group what Lou was doing that seemed to upset everyone. This question unleashed a storm of criticism; every attempt by Lou to deny his fault was met with another accusation. Lou was reduced to tears when the therapist stopped the punishment and pointed out that each person was in the group because of problems, some similar to Lou's. At that point a plan began to evolve in which response costs were attached to teasing behavior and reinforcers were attached to alternate behaviors.

This type of punishment is generally ineffective because of its one-shot nature. To be effective repeated trials are usually called for, but repeated confrontation can be so overwhelming that the therapist risks losing his client.

A less complex form of punishment, but similar to confrontation, is social criticism. Most children find criticism by adults and peers highly aversive. The major problem with its frequent use is that the group itself eventually becomes aversive. However, if the client avoids all criticism he never learns appropriate ways of responding to a common phenomenon. Criticism of specific maladaptive behaviors may be encouraged, but to protect the client from its overuse by his peers, it is used only on the basis of agreements with the group members.

Feedback which indicates merely that the individual is performing the maladaptive behavior can also be considered at least a mild form of punishment. For example, in a group of institutionalized children, the clients agreed that some of their behavior was "crazy": whispering, rocking, screeching, and staring up into the sky. If a child was performing his particular form of "crazy" behavior, the children repeated certain cue words which functioned as aversive stimuli (insofar as they were effective in repressing the behavior). The words used were essentially neutral, such as "orange" when Johnny was rocking. The therapist, in order to train the children in the use of prompting, reinforced the children with a token when they used the agreed-upon cue word.

A physical form of feedback which is mildly embarrassing to the children is also used on occasion. In a group of ten-year olds one child often hit the others. The members believed that rather than being rewarded for periods of nonhitting, he should be required to put on a heavy boxing glove (which served to soften the blows). Since the aggressor agreed, this procedure was accepted by the therapist. A similar procedure was used for a child who screamed all the time. Following each scream the offender was given a surgical mask which he was to wear for thirty seconds (Lindsley, 1966). If the child refuses to follow such a procedure (provided he has previously agreed to it), Lindsley recommends that group stimuli stop until the offender has carried out the behavior.

Although the use of physical punishment has been reported in the behavioral literature on the treatment of autistic children, it is not used in group treatment. Of course it is sometimes bootlegged by the children in the group, who beat a member for something he has done after or even during a meeting. If the therapist does not stop it immediately he is giving his tacit consent. It is not always possible for the therapist to distinguish between contingent and noncontingent fighting and horseplay, and for this reason many therapists immediately make all forms of physical assault off-limits to aggressive children. With passive children, or children who are anxious about physical contact, horseplay and organized fighting may even be reinforced.

Occasionally therapists punish an adaptive behavior by accident. When the therapist arrived five minutes late the room was a shambles. When he questioned the boys, Terry admitted that he had been most responsible for the mess. The therapist then assigned him the task of cleaning the room. Though at first thought this seems appropriate, the therapist was punishing an honesty response, which may not only decrease Terry's future honesty responses but because of the modeling effect may also reduce the other boys' honesty responses.

There is considerable disagreement about the optimal conditions for the administration of punishment procedures. Some authors feel that the dangers of side effects are so great that such procedures should be avoided completely, while others feel that under prescribed conditions they are admissible. I have taken the latter position and have suggested the conditions under which relatively mild punishment procedures can be used with children within the context of the small group.

The application of accelerating and decelerating consequences usually involves contracts and assignments. Their presentation and methods for reaching agreement on their terms are discussed in the following chapter.

8

Contracts and Assignments

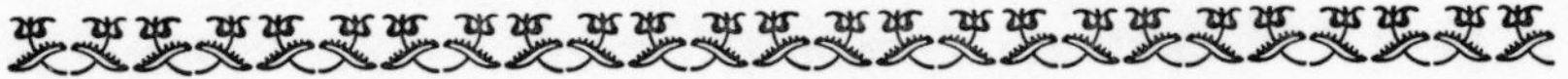

We, the members of the Tigers, agree to discuss in the group our problems at school and at home and to help each other to do something about them. In return Mr. Johnson will provide refreshments, games, trips, and other fun things that aren't too expensive. We shall spend at least as much time talking as doing fun things.

I, Chip S., agree to try to attend school every day this week without cutting class. For every class I attend I get five cents from my mother. If I don't miss any classes, I get a bonus of fifty cents.

These are examples of a treatment contract and a behavioral contract. The treatment contract involves a statement of the general responsibilities of members and therapist over an extended period of time. The behavioral contract is a formal statement of a specific set of agreements—what the client is expected to do over a given time period in return for a given reward.

There is evidence to support the contention that clear knowledge about treatment and agreement to participate are prerequisite for success in treatment (Hoehn-Saric and others, 1964). There is also evidence to link success in learning with knowledge about what one is to learn (Ausubel, 1963) and how one is to learn it (Goldstein, 1966, p. 245). From a practical point of view, because we do not control the major variables in a person's life unless he accepts a given course of action, it is difficult to modify that course of action. From an ethical point of view it is important that early in treatment clients agree to the changes that the therapist will attempt to facilitate and to the means of facilitation. Since all therapies manipulate, a therapeutic approach in which the client knows about and agrees to that manipulation is more acceptable to the individual and society at large.

Knowledge about a situation also reduces the anxiety associated with it. Certainly, many treatment approaches are characterized by a high drop-out or unplanned discontinuance rate. In this approach the drop-out rate is comparatively low. This is probably due in part to the reduction of anxiety produced by the knowledge about the therapist's expectation, and agreement with the therapist's demands and activities. For these reasons this approach is characterized in part by the fact that each member of the group participates actively in determining his own behavioral problem and treatment goals. The group members themselves ultimately decide on group goals and objectives for group meetings. The members are also confronted with the theoretical assumptions of the approach in terms they can understand, and with the procedures to be used to help them attain treatment goals.

Preliminary Treatment Contracts

A set of agreements (the treatment contract) is established early in treatment regarding goals and procedures and the mutual responsibilities of clients, therapist, and the sponsoring agency. These agreements are formally amended from time to time to include new goals and procedures, to add new client or therapist responsibilities, or to modify or reduce these or other areas.

One can identify at least two kinds of treatment contracts—the preliminary and primary treatment contracts. Either may be oral or written, but there is increasing use of the written contracts, especially for the primary contracts. The preliminary type involves only the agreement to take a look at what the group and therapist have to offer. The client can sit in the back of the room; he can participate or not participate as he sees fit; he can attend irregularly. However, he is usually not allowed to be disruptive. This contract is characterized by the absence of any overt verbal commitment to change on the part of the client.

The following example demonstrates an implicit preliminary contract. The eight group members, all early juvenile offenders, were referred to the agency by the police. Although they were reluctant to speak about problems or the behavior that got them into trouble, since it was winter and they had no place else to go they expressed a willingness to meet with the therapist twice a week, to use the agency basketball court, and to eat the food the therapist said he would provide. They also agreed to spend a minimum of fifteen minutes talking to the therapist about what the police had been doing to get them into trouble and to describe what was wrong with their parents. The only commitment on the part of the group members was to talk for a given period in exchange for food and recreational facilities. They indicated that they would use the talking session only to place blame for their problems on others. They made no commitment to work toward change. This situation provided the therapist with an opportunity to present the advantages of such a commitment. Ample use of models during this period, confrontation with the ultimate outcome of their present behavior patterns, ample reinforcement contingent only on coming to meetings, and reinforcement of problem-oriented talk combined to enlist the interest of the group members in making a small commitment to change.

At some point early in treatment the preliminary contract comes to an end. Having observed the possibilities of the group, the client chooses either to remain and develop a more demanding primary contract or to leave the group. Although this limit is made explicit at the beginning of treatment, the shift to a primary contract is often gradual, the client accepting the treatment focus as a useful endeavor without being confronted with a demand for a decision.

The preliminary treatment contract works best with adolescents and, among adolescents, with legal offenders. The discomfort of these clients' maladaptive behaviors and their lack of important skills usually create immediate interest in the prospects offered by the contract.

The most important principle in developing the treatment contract is successive structuring (Rotter, 1954). Because one can not clarify at the first meeting all expectations and procedures for treatment, this is accomplished in a step by step procedure as the group members experience increased satisfaction from the group. The clients are confronted with successively greater demands and more sophisticated explanations: whereas they may have been confronted originally with demands for attendance, participation in discussion and recreational activities, they may be confronted later with the demand to work on specific behavioral changes of their own choosing.

Primary Treatment Contracts

The primary treatment contract is an agreement according to the terms of which the group members work toward behavioral change in exchange for the goods and services provided by the therapist, the agency, and the other group members. Initially only a weak commitment to limited demands is called for, and at this point specific behavioral contracts are developed. Gradually, the demands for change increase as does the participation of the client in the selection of areas requiring change and, eventually, the methods used for achieving it. A good part of every meeting becomes concerned with negotiation of new terms in the treatment and behavioral contracts.

Churchill (1966) describes a secondary treatment contract in which the client not only agrees to work on his own behavior but also agrees to help other members of the group work on their behavior. This particular contract is usually made explicit only after each of the group members has had some success in dealing with his own problems, although the very nature of group reinforcement implies that the conditions of the secondary treatment contract are in operation from the beginning.

Behavioral Contracts

Through behavioral contracts the exact nature of the response-reinforcement contingencies are stated in advance. More specifically, a behavioral contract "is an agreement between two or more persons specifying what each person will do for a stated period of time. It takes the form, I'll do ________ for you, in exchange for your doing ________ for me. A time limit is usually stated or implied. The contract is renegotiable whenever either of the parties to it thinks the terms of the contract are unfair to him" (Krumboltz and Thoresen, 1969, pp. 87–89). Initially, behavior therapists in group treatment negotiated verbal agreements with their clients, but as evidence accrued that the unwritten contracts were often ambiguous, misunderstood, ignored, or forgotten, the trend has been to written contracts.

> During the next two group meetings, for every ten minute period that I, Jon, work or play together with another person without fighting or yelling, I will receive one token from Dr. Carter. If there is any disagreement about what constitutes fighting or yelling, the group will decide by majority vote. Dr. Carter will provide me with a kitchen timer which I will set every ten minutes.

________	________	________
Jon	Dr. Carter	Date

Behavioral contracts are more specific than treatment contracts and usually are more limited in time. Treatment contracts cover the general rules of operation; behavioral contracts cover what the client or group of clients will do next week or in the next two days to achieve specific consequences. All treatment contracts are group contracts insofar as they posit expectations for all members and the therapist. Behavioral contracts may be made either for individuals or the group. The individual contracts posit specific individual behaviors in exchange for individual consequences whereas a group behavioral contract calls for group or subgroup performance in exchange for a group reward. It should be noted that group treatment contracts and group behavioral contracts differ only in degree, and it is possible to conceive of borderline cases which could be correctly assigned to either category.

> For the next month, all members of the Rangers will look for jobs. This means that every person will apply to at least two employment agencies, make an appointment, and hold at least one employment interview. In addition each person is responsible for reading the want ads and reporting at the group meeting all jobs requiring less than a high school education. At each meeting the members will fill in an hourly time card for all activities mentioned above, including the group meeting, and will be paid at the rate of twenty-five cents an hour. Mr. Brown has the right and obligation to check to see whether interviews were held and whether each boy tried to get a job. Applications will be filled in during the group meetings so that Mr. Brown can help.

Because of the extensiveness as well as the specificity of this contract it serves as both a treatment and group behavioral contract. If it should appear that the clients do not know exactly what they are to receive or what they are to do, a more specific contract would need to be developed.

A group behavioral contract is similar to an individual one except that it pertains to group rather than individual contingencies and must be negotiated with the entire group rather than one individual. The reason for such a contract is that on occasion individual members have tried to keep to the terms of their contract only to be seduced away from it by other members. Because group pressure keeps them all in line, there has been increasing use of the group contract. Just as in the individual contract, it is necessary to make the conditions as clear as possible since most clients exhibit unusual legal talent in finding loopholes in the contract.

It is in negotiating the contract that client participation has its greatest impact. This does not mean that clients get whatever they want. Neither does it mean that the therapist can do whatever he wants.

In negotiating the behavioral contract, clients are afforded the first opportunity to state what they would like to change. This reduces the likelihood of their feeling pressured by the therapist. If a client has no suggestions of his own, the other group members are asked for recommendations and only if they have no suggestions will the therapist propose behaviors to be worked on. If at all possible he will recommend alternatives, so that a choice of legitimate targets is available to the client. The same process occurs in determining rewards or other consequences. Each client is asked, "Is this fair? Is this achievable in the given time period? Do you know exactly what has to be done?" The therapist may then suggest hypothetical occurrences which might interfere with the client's performance during the given time period. Most of the work is carried out between meetings; the meeting is a laboratory in which the client learns new behaviors or how to control old ones, to negotiate contracts, and to prepare for the work to be performed between meetings.

Behavioral Assignments

A behavioral assignment is another type of contract which involves work to be done between meetings. Assignments are directly related to the treatment goal and may represent a subgoal or intermediate goal. Since stimulus conditions for many behaviors do not occur within a treatment group, the assignment is an excellent means of extending treatment into the extratherapeutic situation. The effectiveness of behavioral assignments depends on a number of factors. First, the assignment must be highly specific; if certain unexpected conditions arise or if the stimulus conditions do not occur, alternative behaviors, such as calling the therapist, should be specified. If the assignment is too vague, the client can hedge, the monitoring becomes difficult, and the effectiveness of the endeavor can scarcely be estimated. Second, the stimulus conditions for the assignment should have a relatively high probability of occurring. Third, some form of reinforcement should follow successful completion of the task. Ideally, reinforcement should follow as soon as possible after the response one wishes to obtain. Yet reinforcement of behavioral assignments usually occurs at the group meeting, considerably after the performance of the desired behaviors. There are several ways to deal with this delay. The therapist may ask the behavior monitors to reinforce the client on the spot with tokens or praise. When behaviors must increase or decrease over a given time period, the therapist may design the assignment in such a way that the fixed interval terminates at exactly the moment the group meeting begins. If this arrangement is not feasible, a special meeting may be held in the middle of the week to distribute reinforcement or the therapist may telephone the client or have the client telephone him when the assignment is completed.

If tokens or other rewards are given for successful completion of an assignment, monitoring by direct observation or the report of a significant other is desirable. The therapist otherwise may be put in a position of reinforcing exaggerated accounts or lies. If monitoring is impossible or if monitors are unreliable or uncooperative, reinforcement should not be used.

If the client states that he is unable to perform a given assignment because he does not understand what he should do, is frightened or uncomfortable, the therapist can reduce his discomfort in a number of ways. He may discuss the behavior with the other members of the group, especially those who have already performed it under the stipulated conditions. He may demonstrate or ask one of the group to demonstrate exactly how the assignment is to be performed. He may use behavioral rehearsal prior to which he or a peer models the behavior to be performed (see following chapter). The therapist may modify the environment so that the probability of success is increased. For a child whose mother criticized him unmercifully whether or not he changed, the therapist arranged for a sympathetic uncle, whose presence had already proved ameliorative, to sit in the house during the week assignments were to be done. It also appears that if group members develop assignments for each other, there is increased agreement to the assignments and a higher probability of successful completions.

Normally, an assignment should not be an isolated event but one of a series, each of which more closely approximates the terminal goal. After an assignment is successfully completed in a variety of relevant situations, a slightly more difficult one should be given. Each assignment should be sufficiently difficult that the client must make some effort to accomplish it, but sufficiently within his reach that success is highly probable. As previously noted, success in change is a potent reinforcement for attempting change in the future. If performing the assignment requires no change at all, it reinforces behaviors which are already in the client's repertoire. This reinforcement may be necessary for a short period of time to stabilize change, but if the client remains at one phase too long, he may become bored or annoyed with the activity.

The following sequence of assignments was originally developed for a group of children (ages ten and eleven) who lacked appropriate approach and other social responses to other children. Most of these children had been referred because they had no friends and complained of being unhappy or depressed. This sequence has been used with minor variations in several groups because of the prevalence of the problem.

The first assignment is to greet a child in school the next day with, "Hi, how're you" or a similar remark. The child should be someone the client likes but to whom he has not spoken before. In preparation for the assignment the group discusses how children in their neighborhood address one another and decides on the best expression to use. Assertive members of the group demonstrate and the others practice (making sure an appropriate tone of voice and eye contact are used). The monitoring procedure is a self-report in which the child describes to the group what happened. The child also calls another group member as soon as the assignment has been attempted. The criteria for success are the attempt and the description of it (since no validating source exists, completion is not required). The alternative, if the child finds the task too difficult, is to address one member of the group in school. This assignment may seem very easy, but for many children it involves a tremendous effort. In fact, some form of desensitization in imagination may have to precede the attempt.

The second assignment is to greet a child whom the client likes and to talk briefly to him. In preparation for the assignment, the group discusses possible topics of conversation. Each member chooses at least two topics of interest to him and the children demonstrate and rehearse. They discuss possible responses by the other person and what to do if he ignores the client, gets angry, or becomes talkative and friendly. Some pointers on how to get away are given. The monitoring procedures and criteria for success are the same as for the first assignment.

The third assignment is to approach other children, ask them to play a game the client knows, and play the game. In preparation for the assignment the children learn games such as checkers and Parcheesi, which they practice in the group meeting. They discuss and demonstrate good-loser and good-winner behavior and for purposes of discrimination play at both. Each member chooses a game he wants to play and is provided with materials. This assignment is repeated several times. When possible more than one other person is included and several different games are played.

The fourth assignment is to teach and play a new game with someone else. In preparation the game is taught to group members. Each one rehearses teaching it to the others, they again discuss winner and loser behaviors, and review their experiences with the previous assignment. Variations of this assignment are to teach games involving cooperative or team behaviors and to help another child with his homework.

A similar series has been developed in relation to the teacher, for use when there has been a lack of positive communication. The first assignment is to say "good morning" to the teacher in an appropriate tone of voice. Preparation is discussion, demonstration, and rehearsal in group meetings, and use of a tape recorder to practice correct tone. The second assignment is to ask a question in class in an appropriate manner. Again, the tape-recorder can be used, especially in confronting overly assertive children and those who speak in an irritating manner with their present behaviors. A further "rub-in" can be obtained by asking other children how they would respond to the given child if they were the teacher. Shy or withdrawn children can view a role-play demonstration by their peers. The third assignment is to answer a question by the teacher when the child knows the answer and when he does not. Preparation is the same as for the second assignment and in addition the therapist may enlist the cooperation of the teacher to ensure success. The fourth assignment is for the client to discuss in some detail a problem in class. Gradually the complexity of the problem can be increased. Preparation is the same as for the second assignment.

Most referred children lack cooperative behaviors. These may be encouraged by assigning the child to help another with a specific list of spelling words (or arithmetic problems) in which the first child has at least some skill. This task involves giving him a specific set of instructions (or involving him in developing these instructions), helping the client to learn necessary teaching skills, and praising him when something is done well. Role-play can help train the child to cope with failure.

In each of these examples the reader should note that a large number of procedures have been used to prepare the child for completion of his behavioral assignment. Some of these procedures are successive approximation, reinforcement, and the use of contracts. Another set of procedures, such as the use of a tape recorder and role-playing, is also suggested. These are described in detail in the next chapter under the rubrics of modeling and behavioral rehearsal.

9

Modeling and Behavioral Rehearsal

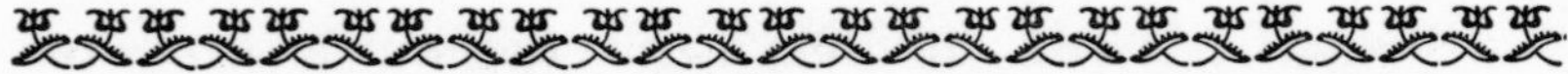

Warren, the oldest and most admired member of the group, announced to the other members that he had just been hired as a delivery boy at the corner grocery. Up to now none of the others in the group had exhibited an interest in earning—as opposed to stealing—their pocket money, but during the week that followed Everet, Brian, and Freddie applied for jobs as newsboys.

Debbie and Gabrielle never talked in class. In fact, no one could remember that they had ever asked a question. The group members decided to pretend that the group was a class, the therapist was the teacher, and the two girls were given questions they could ask. Whenever they faltered the other girls prompted them.

In the first example the behavior of group members is altered by observing that of an older and admired child. In the second, the members try to alter the behavior of their group mates by having them role-play what they should do in the classroom. The first is an example of modeling, the second of behavioral rehearsal. Although they are used independently in the examples, modeling and behavioral rehearsal are usually combined as a means of preparing clients to perform their behavior assignments.

A major means of acquiring new behavioral patterns is through the observation of the behavior and its consequences. Bandura (1969, pp. 118–216) cites extensive research demonstrating that one can acquire intricate motor responses and emotional reactions, or extinguish fearful or avoidant responses, through such observation. This form of learning involves an observer and a model. A modeling procedure is a set of therapist activities designed to increase the observer's probability of matching behavior. Modeling procedures include introducing potential models, pointing out behavior to be imitated, modifying situational conditions to facilitate imitation, teaching observational and imitational skills, reinforcment, and role-playing. Modeling procedures, which lend themselves especially to the group treatment situation, represent a major set of therapist interventions. A group contains an abundance of potential models, new models can be introduced without seriously disrupting existing social patterns, and multi-person role-playing can readily be utilized. Group pressures can be stimulated to encourage imitation.

Although modeling is seldom isolated from reinforcement procedures, behavioral rehearsal, and behavioral assignments, I am concerned here only with the prerequisites of imitation, principles for increasing the probability of imitation, types of models, and techniques for the presentation of models. The theoretical basis of the chapter is found, for the most part, in Bandura (1969), and the purpose here is to apply the theory to treatment of children within the context of the small group.

Prerequisites for Imitation

One necessary condition of imitation is an attending response to the model's behavior. One obviously cannot imitate what he does not perceive. Frequently, therefore, it is necessary to teach children how to attend to models before it is possible to encourage imitation.

In some cases, the client has sufficient observational skills but fails to observe the behaviors most useful to him. In order to facilitate greater discrimination, the therapist may instruct the client to look for specific model behaviors and their outcomes, or he may develop a specific observational schedule with the group members and train them in its use.

Clients will usually display a wide variety of matching skills. Because younger children (ages four to eight) seem to have the greatest deficit in this area a number of procedures have been used with younger groups to increase imitative skill. One set of techniques involves the group members in games in which the members must, singly or in unison, imitate the therapist or each other. One game in particular—"Who am I?"—involves each member in imitating a social or task role—such as father, basketball player, old man, carpenter. The rest of the group attempts to determine who the client is. Although this is a relatively easy game for most children, many clients must be trained to play the role by demonstration and prompting.

In another game the therapist tells a story whose words and actions the group members must repeat. (This also gives them practice in instructional control.) The therapist first makes brief, discrete motor movements and as the members become skilled in these, he moves to longer and more complex sets of behaviors. Eventually the therapist replaces himself as leader with one of the members, whom the rest of the group must imitate. A timer can be used to increase the time between action and imitative reaction and affords practice in retention as well as imitation. Some therapists may reward the group initially for successful imitation—usually on a fixed interval schedule of reinforcement—but for most groups, the rewards inherent in the game are sufficient.

This activity is frequently utilized in the very first group meeting of younger children because the therapist can assure success by controlling the difficulty of the activity. Moreover, since the children appear to enjoy it, the attractiveness of the group is enhanced and group members are involved in non-threatening common play, a first step in the process of peer interaction.

Characteristics of Effective Models

The extent to which a client matches behavior is in part a function of certain characteristics of the model. Some attributes which may increase the probability are the high rewarding potential of the model; demonstration by the model of competence in areas highly regarded by the observer; and general renown or relatively high social power in respect to the observer. In my experience the models usually need to show some of the observer's population attributes (race, history of delinquency, youth, sex) in addition to these characteristics. Except in the case of celebrities, models must be able to project themselves as possessors of a skill or status which the client could realistically expect to achieve himself. In a series of field studies in summer camp by Lippitt, Polansky, Redl, and Rosen (1952) the authors found that more children imitate the high-power than the low-power child. This was true of "contaged," or spontaneous, imitation in which no influence attempts were used, as well as conforming behavior which the high-power person attempted to bring about. Power was determined primarily on the basis of sociometric questionnaires on which the children designated who was "the best at getting others to do what he wants them to do." The implication for group treatment is that models should be regarded as powerful people by the group members. "Power" can refer to the potential of the individual to distribute relevant rewards and punishment. I have used as models for groups of juvenile offenders individuals who had at least several of the above characteristics. For example, for boys' groups I have used reformed delinquents who were employed, slightly more athletic than the clients, and had been but were no longer members of high status gangs in the neighborhood.

Since dependency on the model by the client has been shown to increase the probability of imitation, (Bandura, 1969, p. 137) in early group meetings the therapist can foster the client's dependency by maintaining a high degree of structure in the group, by assisting members with physical assistance of all sorts where needed, by direct advice when asked for, and so forth. Of course, as treatment progresses, independence from the therapist and models is taught in preparation for leaving the group.

Incentives for Imitation

Although clients tend to imitate certain models more readily than others, as Bandura points out (1969, p. 137), "incentive control of observing behaviors in most instances overrides the effects of variation in observer characteristics and model attributes." It is for this reason that modeling is frequently combined with reinforcement procedures. Reinforcement of the model increases the likelihood that the client will match the model's behavior. This is especially effective if the model is rewarded in the presence of the imitator; however, it is usually sufficient if the imitator only has knowledge of the reward (see Bandura, 1969, p. 128). It appears also that the frequency of matching responses is reduced when the model is directly or vicariously punished (Bandura, 1969, p. 128), although research on this is slight.

In the following example, the therapist first reinforces the model and then the imitators: Most of the group members were running around the room. Alice was sitting quietly and talking to Mary Ann, who was leaning against the counter. The therapist ostentatiously gave both girls a token. The rest of the girls trickled back to the table; as they arrived each was awarded a token.

Since the behavior to be imitated was relatively simple there was little doubt that each girl could duplicate it. More overt attempts at instructional control, however, might have resulted in a power struggle between the therapist and the newly formed group.

In the following example, Frank, a high-status group member, initiates a new trend in the conversation. The therapist reinforces the whole group for the behavior of the model. Note that there is a delayed "contagion" in this case.

Frank began to talk about the trouble the truant officer was giving him. He said (first time such a statement had been made in the group) that he guessed he was "back-talking" too much. The therapist chalked up five points on the group thermometer. The group members looked at each other and the therapist but continued to run down truant officers and the police. In about ten minutes, however, the conversation moved to a discussion of what each did to irritate parents, teachers, and the police.

Although the verbal behavior which the therapist wanted to increase was relatively specific, the members did not respond until it was clear that reinforcement was not forthcoming for any behavior other than problem talk. Although they may have been manipulating the therapist in order to obtain the reward, even practice in giving "lip service" is an important step prior to changing the behavior.

In the following example a more complex set of behaviors are imitated. Although each member of the group had tried at least once to obtain a job, they all had failed and behavior appeared to have been extinguished. Frank had expressed an interest in finding a job on several recent occasions and the therapist prepared him for an interview through behavioral rehearsal. In addition, the therapist arranged a job in advance to insure success and reinforcement of the model.

Frank, accompanied by the therapist and group members, went to the news agency to get a job as a newsboy. Frank went in the building alone while the others waited impatiently. Ten minutes later Frank came out with a big smile. He had the job. In the course of the next month three other boys tried to get jobs and two of them were successful. During that period there was a great deal of discussion and training on how to get jobs.

In each of these examples, a great deal is done in addition to rewarding the model in the presence of other group members. Although it is quite possible that any one of these actions would have been sufficient to obtain matched responses from the others, the clinician needs to utilize the optimal combination of established principles in order to maximize the probability of success.

Of major relevance, because it occurred within a group context, is a study carried out by Hawkins (1964). Although his subjects were adult schizophrenic patients, one can readily extrapolate to a treatment situation involving juvenile offenders. The dependent variable was the rate of affectively-toned verbal statements occurring during the group treatment sessions. Three conditions were created: in the first patient-models avoided the use of the affectively-toned statements; in the second the patient-models frequently used such words; and in the third no patient-models were present. In all three cases the therapist reinforced all affectively-toned statements. The results indicated that modeling plus reinforcement increased the frequency of the desired statements far more than either of the other two conditions. In fact, when models were present but did not emit the given statements, the frequency significantly diminished from the original baseline.

As Bandura (1969, p. 136) points out, "Modeled characteristics that are highly discernible can be more readily acquired than subtle attributes which must be abstracted from heterogeneous responses differing on numerous stimulus dimensions." This does not imply that complex stimuli can not be learned, but that a complex instructional approach is often required which utilizes combinations of hierarchical modeling, reinforcement of successive approximations, and other techniques. Furthermore, if the behavioral repertoire of the client is impoverished, his matching skill may be grossly deficient because he lacks the necessary components of the behavior to be matched. In these cases, complex behavior patterns should be broken down into smaller units, which are modeled separately and reinforced appropriately. In addition, behavioral rehearsal, either covert or overt, can be used to facilitate retention of the initially-modeled behavior.

Peers, Therapists, and Guests as Models

Having investigated some of the principles for optimizing matching, let us look at model sources. The first source is the other members of the group. However, most groups in treatment consist of individuals who have failed to perform in satisfying ways or who perform only antisocial norms successfully. This is especially true in groups whose members have similar problems: the members repeatedly observe their peers' maladaptive patterns, which are intermittently reinforced and thus maintained. Only the therapist seems to perform differently and his characteristics—high level of education, middle class, and deviant (from the culture of the group)—initially mitigate against enthusiastic imitation.

The implications are that group members should manifest a wide range of both maladaptive and adaptive patterns of social relations and that as the group progresses members should be added who manifest the desired adaptive patterns.

But peers are not the only source of models. In an often quoted statement, Mowrer (1966) has noted that clinicians characteristically present themselves as models for a very limited range of social behavior, and what they do demonstrate usually has limited application for their clients. Although this appears to be especially valid in the evocative therapies, where the clinician is taciturn and interpretive, I suspect a similar criticism could be made of many behavioral therapists. In order to facilitate the therapist's role as model, he is encouraged to demonstrate in anecdote or role-play how he deals with (selected) stress situations which he encounters. If the home situation of the therapist is not too foreign to the group members, they can be invited to spend time with him and his family. The group members are encouraged to observe the therapist in social situations similar to those with which they themselves are confronted. In the group meetings the therapist discusses the problems he is coping with openly and spontaneously as a means of encouraging similar openness and spontaneity on the part of his clients. This is not inconsistent with the earlier statement that peer-related models may be more effective. I subscribe to the dictum, the more (models) the merrier and the greater the likelihood that the client will find adequate models for his several purposes. The direction seems to be a promising one. Clients seem able to determine more readily what they must do in treatment and they appear to be more attracted to the therapist whose actions are consistent with his expectations.

An interesting experiment occurred as a result of the children's complaint that the therapist got them to do what he wanted but did not always do what they wanted. The therapist suggested that they discuss one of his behaviors that they did not like and that as a group they should try to change it. Much to his chagrin the members pointed out that he often interrupted and on occasion did not seem to be listening to what they were saying. As a group they designed a system of monitoring his behavior by assigning one member as observer every ten minutes. The observer would count the number of times the therapist appeared not to be listening and another member would count the therapist's interruptions. After two meetings a baseline of eight interruptions and five occurrences of nonlistening had been established. The group decided that they would give feedback to the therapist by turning on a flashlight whenever the behavior occurred. The result was a complete elimination of interruptions and only an occasional occurrence of nonlistening after two weeks of flashlight treatment.

When the therapist provided himself as a model for appropriate client behavior (by admitting that all his behaviors were *not* those of a model), he showed the group how to present problematic behaviors and encouraged them to devise ways of changing his behavior. This appeared to increase both his attractiveness as a person and his clients' readiness to deal with their problems.

Another model source is the paid guest who is particularly attractive to the group members. The models are programed to discuss the "moral dilemmas" with which they were confronted in their adolescence and how they resolved these in a prosocial way. Athletes, for example, can also reward the group by giving the members lessons.

Another example was the addition to a group of juvenile offenders of two "reformed" delinquents who held jobs, drove old cars, and had girl friends. Held in high esteem by the members, these ex-delinquents were hired as assistant therapists and in general performed the physical and verbal behaviors which the therapist wanted to be emulated. The group members were aware of their special status as assistants and later, when several new members were added to the group, some old members were shifted to the paid assistant role.

One could envision an ongoing treatment group in which distinct roles were enunciated: initiate, regular working member, paid model, and even a trained community group aide role in which a former group member assumed other leadership functions in the group. Each role would have different contractual arrangements attached to it in terms of expected performance, and rewards for conformity to expectations. This would provide a broad basis for models and jobs for successful "graduates." It is quite similar to Fairweather's (1964) model in a mental hospital.

Such models are far more potent than the therapist or parents. The implication for treatment is that models need to be used who have population and subcultural characteristics similar to the street heroes but who also have certain adaptive behaviors in their repertoire.

Procedures for Presentation of Models

If the client does not seem attracted to any member of the group or his goal behavior is not within the other members' repertoires, the client is usually asked to describe in specific behavioral terms someone he admires who seems to be successful (Kelly, 1955). If he can not be specific, he is encouraged to watch that person carefully during the week and note behaviors which seem to lead to the outcomes the client would also like to experience. Of course, one runs the chance that the client may choose a decidedly delinquent or neurotic model. In these cases, the client may be encouraged to observe ultimate negative outcomes.

When the client has a picture of the pattern of behavior, he describes it to the therapist and group members. Repeated observation is usually required before his description is sufficiently detailed to warrant imitation. At this point the therapist may utilize a rehearsal procedure followed by an assignment to try out the procedures.

Harry liked girls but only swore at them or hit them, and as a result they avoided him. When he asked the other members what he did, they told him, but they couldn't offer any good alternatives. Harry was instructed by several members to watch King, the star athlete in his eighth grade class, as he talked to girls, who as a rule liked King. Chuck decided he'd watch, too. Each of the boys was required by their peers to bring back a detailed report to the group the following week. At the next meeting Harry and Chuck described what King did and said. It appeared that King occasionally complimented the girls and often asked them questions. The therapist encouraged the two boys, one at a time, to play the role of King, while he, the therapist, played the role of the girls. The group members were asked to comment on the success of the players in duplicating King's behavior. In spite of great initial hilarity, the role play became quite serious as the members carefully instructed the role players how to play their roles effectively. It appeared that they all had been observing King during the course of the week.

Models also can be taped, videotaped, or filmed. These are especially useful in treatment groups with no adequate models. In groups involved in verbal therapy, Truax, Carkhuff, and Kodman (1965) had one set of clients listen to tapes exemplifying good self-exploration prior to treatment. A control group had no such preparation. After the two groups underwent the same treatment it was discovered that the experimental group displayed greater change on a variety of personality tests.

A self-modeling procedure using a videotape has been reported by Creer and Miklich (1970) in the treatment of Chuck, a ten-year old asthmatic boy. As a patient in a residential treatment home, he spent most of his time watching television or reading. He was rebuffed in his attempts to join in the activities of other children with teasing and name-calling to which he responded with temper tantrums. When with adults, he giggled a lot and manifested such silly behaviors as jumping from chair to chair and onto the adult's lap. Since Chuck overslept every morning, he seldom made his bed or tidied his room. In order to treat the behavior, two tapes were developed.

> The first tape displayed inappropriate behavioral chains. Here, Chuck behaved in his usual manner. Briefly, the scenes showed: (1) Chuck remaining in bed when the light was turned on in the morning; (2) Chuck exhibiting a temper tantrum when assaulted by two boys; (3) Chuck being rejected by two boys with whom he asked to play; and (4) Chuck entering an office and jumping on the lap of an adult. All of the scenes were rehearsed beforehand to obtain authenticity. That Chuck's responses were realistic was demonstrated by the fact that he bruised his hand striking a table in the second scene.
>
> Tape two showed appropriate behavioral chains. In these four scenes, Chuck was shown: (1) promptly getting out of bed in the morning, dressing and making his bed; (2) physically defending himself and repulsing an attack by two other boys; (3) appropriately initiating contacts with two peers when the latter were playing a game; and (4) entering an office and interacting in an appropriate manner with an adult. Again, all scenes were rehearsed to obtain verisimilitude [p. 51].

The tapes were viewed daily for alternating two-week periods. During the periods that the appropriate behaviors were shown, Chuck's appropriate behaviors increased; during the inappropriate periods, Chuck's inappropriate behaviors increased. Where videotape is available, this procedure seems to be a promising one, especially for the child whose initial relations with the group are so disturbed that his opportunities to observe peer behavior are limited to the occasions when he is the target of their aggression.

In order to help the client focus on specific behaviors which he must learn to match, role-playing is frequently used. When observing the natural model the client may have to wait a long time before the behaviors to be emulated appear. Role-playing permits the client to observe a narrow range of behaviors in repeated situations over a short period of time. In this form of role playing, the model plays the client's role. The client may either play the role of the "significant-other" or coach the person who plays that role and he usually acts as "director" for the entire skit. The clients (usually there are several in a group situation who have the same or similar concerns) are instructed to observe specific actions of the person playing their role and to be prepared to discuss how it is different from what they do in their own situations.

In order to insure that the desired behaviors are performed, the person playing the client's role may be instructed in how to play it. Instruction frequently occurs in subgroups: all members are assigned to one or another subgroup and each subgroup is assigned a role. The client is assigned to a subgroup preparing to portray a parent, teacher, or other person with whom he is concerned. The roles are then spelled out in some detail by the subgroups. It is useful for the subgroups, not the therapist, to choose not only the person to play the role but an alternate as well. The alternate may also act as a "conscience" or prompter. Use of subgroups results in greater involvement of all members and tends to reduce resistance to role-playing.

Quite often, the therapist, group aide, or paid guest will be the first person to play the role of the client; he is followed by a group member or several group members who are instructed in the subgroup, and finally the client rehearses his own role, which includes the new behaviors he has observed. Variability in models offers the client greater choice of behavior styles and increases the probability of stabilization of the behavior once it is learned. (See Chapter Fourteen.)

Previously mentioned principles for increasing probability of matched responses are also applicable in role-played model presentation. If possible the model should be rewarded during the role-play or immediately following it. If peers are used, high status group members should be used. Prior to the role-playing, the client may also be given specific observational instructions.

Sarason and Ganzer (1969) used written scripts for modeling and behavioral rehearsal procedures as the major form of interventions with groups of institutionalized delinquents. They agree with the observations of many others (for example, Bandura and Walters, 1963) that delinquents frequently are characterized by a history of inadequate and unfortunate modeling experiences. Most delinquents' models have been antisocial adults or older delinquent adolescents. The purpose of the project was to demonstrate the effectiveness of establishing new, socially acceptable, and, hopefully, exciting social models for the delinquent.

In a series of sessions, social models—usually graduate students in clinical psychology—role-played situations which the adolescents were likely to encounter following discharge from the institution: obtaining employment, building self-control, planning ahead, discussing rules at home with parents, dealing with group pressure to commit delinquent acts, handling testing in social situations, taking responsibility, getting help for school problems, and apologizing when appropriate. The procedures for each session are described below:

> Each session is attended by six persons, two models and four boys. One complete scene is used for each meeting. Each meeting follows a sequence:
>
> a) one model introduces and describes the scene for the day;
>
> b) models role-play the scripts while the boys observe;
>
> c) one boy is called upon to summarize and explain the content and outcome of the situation;
>
> d) models comment and discuss the scene, then replay the recording;
>
> e) pairs of boys imitate and rehearse the roles and behaviors;
>
> f) a short "break" is taken, while soft drinks are served and one of the two role-playing imitations is replayed;
>
> g) the remaining boys act out the scene;
>
> h) one of these two performances is replayed; and, finally,
>
> i) final summaries and comments concerning the scene, aspects of its importance, and general applicability are emphasized [p. 190].

As part of this study the modeling group and matched

control (untreated) group were compared in terms of changes on a semantic differential and the Wahler Self-Description Inventory. It was discovered that modeling groups became more dissatisfied with themselves personally while the control groups became more satisfied with themselves. The experimental groups also showed more change in behavior and attitudes than the control group.

The modeling, too, involved a great deal of physical activity. In the skits, the therapists encouraged the boys to stand up and move about the room. This would appear to be vastly superior to having teenagers sit passively in their chairs, especially if, as the writers point out, delinquent boys are primarily action or movement oriented rather than verbally oriented. The authors observe that the boys' attention span was about twenty to thirty minutes and that breaks were taken in mid-session because of this.

In general, it might have been better to use less academic and lower socioeconomic class models. As I pointed out earlier, if the discrepancy between the model and the observer is too great in terms of these variables, imitation is less likely to occur. The increase in self-dissatisfaction in the experimental group is a confusing finding but not necessarily a negative one and may suggest that the technique raised more questions about the boys' personal adequacy than it pointed to specific solutions to their problems. Revisions like those suggested above and the use of methods supplementing the social modeling approach should result in a still more powerful treatment tool.

As I pointed out earlier, if the model is punished for performance of a given set of behaviors, the likelihood of imitation may be diminished. Based on this principle, role-playing of a model involved in antisocial behavior and its negative outcome should serve to diminish the probability that the client will match the model's behavior. Actually, in my experience such role-plays primarily afford the therapist an opportunity to introduce discussion of maladaptive behaviors and effective and adaptive alternatives. They can also serve as a form of discrimination training in which the adaptive and maladaptive behaviors are portrayed back to back in order to see which is more effective.

Behavioral Rehearsal

Having observed the model, the client must imitate his behavior. But before he attempts to utilize a complex sequence of new behaviors in his daily environment, it is frequently desirable for him to try them out in the treatment situation. Here the therapist or clients play the role of significant others and the given client plays his own role. This use of role-playing is called behavioral rehearsal (Lazarus, 1966). Its purpose is to provide the client with practice in a protected situation so that he will be less anxious in the real one and more likely to succeed. Since practice is viewed in most nontherapeutic situations as a sina qua non for learning, it seems equally valid to use practice to promote the learning of social behaviors.

Behavioral rehearsal differs from role-played model presentation in that someone else demonstrates to the client how he should play his role. Behavioral rehearsal is usually preceded by model presentation, advice, or a simple description of what the client should do in a given situation. It is usually followed by a behavioral assignment to try out the new behaviors—or at least some of them—in the client's broader environment. The advantages of behavioral rehearsal as a therapeutic technique have been discussed by Sturm (1965, p. 57), who suggests that behavioral rehearsal in comparison to other techniques has "a far greater potential to 1) generate vivid, life-like behavior and cues, thereby maximizing the utility of response and stimulus generalization; 2) condition a *total* behavioral response—physiological, motoric, and ideational—rather than one merely verbal, and 3) dispense the powerful reinforcements of enacted models and other characters, who in real life or in fantasy have already dispensed reinforcements." Sturm also notes that the skillful application of flexible techniques such as behavioral rehearsal helps to create near-veridical behavior while focusing on the problem at hand, thereby facilitating the patient's ease and efficiency in participating and learning.

Another source of support for the use of behavioral rehearsal is the findings of Underwood and Schulz (1960, p. 86) who conclude that "other things being equal, therefore, the more frequently a verbal unit has been experienced the more quickly this will become a response in a new associations connection." Drawing upon similar research findings, Goldstein and others (1966, p. 236) strongly urge that "desired responses should be emphasized and practiced during the therapy sessions."

Although it is usually difficult to examine an isolated technique empirically, there are a number of experiments in which the efficacy of behavioral rehearsal has been systematically examined. Lazarus (1966), comparing behavioral rehearsal to nondirective therapy and advice-giving treatment, found that behavioral rehearsal was by far the most effective method of resolving specific social and interpersonal problems. He assigned seventy-five outpatients to three treatment conditions: behavioral rehearsal, reflection-interpretation, and direct advice. One problem only was treated in each of the three conditions in four weekly sessions of thirty minutes. If there was no evidence of change or learning within the month, the treatment was regarded as a failure. The criterion of change was objective evidence that the patient was performing adaptively in the area which had previously constituted a problem.

The results showed that 32 per cent and 44 per cent of the patients, respectively, benefited from reflection-interpretation and advice and 92 per cent benefited from behavioral rehearsal. Of the thirty-one patients who did not benefit from reflection-interpretation and advice, twenty-seven were later treated with behavioral rehearsal, twenty-two successfully.

In a carefully designed experiment, Wagner (1968) found that reinforcement of role-played expressions of anger resulted in an increase in the expression of anger among mildly inhibited hospitalized patients. In this study he divided twenty-nine patients into three treatment groups which were equated on the basis of scores on an anger-expression test. In the experimental group subjects were encouraged to express anger in role-played situations. All expressions of anger in the role play were reinforced in the sense that the "other" submitted to their anger and, if appropriate, apologized for giving cause for anger. In a contrast group the "other" retaliated with greater anger than the subject had expressed. In a control group expression of anger was neither encouraged nor reinforced nor punished.

The results showed significantly greater expression of anger for the experimental group, with no significant change in the control or contrast group.

In a study by McFall and Marston (1970), two behavioral rehearsal treatment conditions were compared to a placebo and a control group. One of the experimental conditions involved a feedback procedure to the subject; the second did not. All subjects had requested help in becoming more assertive in their social relationships. Tested on four different instruments, the experimental conditions resulted in significantly greater assertiveness than either the placebo or control condition. There was no significant difference between the two experimental conditions although the behavior rehearsal with feedback showed a somewhat stronger effect.

Prior to setting up a behavioral rehearsal in the group, the therapist and the members must isolate the behavior which needs to be performed and the conditions under which it should appropriately occur. Whenever possible, behaviors which are not (but should be) in the repertoire of *most* of the members are chosen. Obviously, these behaviors are closely linked to the treatment goals. Next, the behavior to be performed must be demonstrated either in discussion or role-play (model presentation).

Anxiety about the rehearsal itself may be reduced if the client first reviews verbally what he is going to say and if he knows someone else will prompt him if he forgets responses during the rehearsal. Prompting by group members appears to be more effective than prompting by the therapist, but self-manipulated prompts such as cue cards are still better since the client can use these in the real as well as in the role-played situation.

After the client performs the role-play the other members make suggestions as to how it could be altered—the conditions under which the client's responses were inappropriate—

and discuss possible consequences of the client's actions. Finally, the client and other group members are given behavioral assignments to try out the newly acquired behaviors in the actual situations with which the client is learning to cope.

In the following example a sequence of model presentation, behavioral rehearsal, behavioral assignments, and monitoring is demonstrated. The reader should note that the therapist encourages many short trials, increases the difficulty of the situation, and reduces the reinforcers given by the "significant other."

> Jane, a recent high school graduate, had just been refused employment on two job interviews. Being rather timid and nonassertive, Jane was disappointed and on the verge of crying when she came to the group meeting. She stated that there was another job-opening in her neighborhood but she was fearful of being rejected a third time. Jane's closest friend, Mabel, was also in the group. Mabel was already working. At the suggestion of the therapist she was willing to play the part of job applicant and the therapist played the employer's part. Jane was told to watch closely as Mabel played her (Jane's) part. Mabel played the part well and the therapist asked Jane first to review exactly what Mabel did. With some hesitation Jane then began her rehearsal by saying, 'I saw the "girl wanted" sign in the window.' But when she was asked if she could work until seven, Jane appeared tense and offered no response. When Louise prompted her with some suggestions, Jane was better able to answer and after practice with more unexpected questions, Jane gradually became more comfortable. The therapist responded initially with smiles and compliments to her assertive responses but gradually became more businesslike and less pleasant. At the last trial the group applauded her efforts and Jane beamed. Jane's behavioral assignment was to apply for the job the next day. The therapist announced to Jane that he expected her to report on the outcome of the interview at the next meeting. She was relieved to know that if the interview did not work she could continue practicing for other interviews.

An interesting variation of behavioral rehearsal has been described by Gittelman (1965, pp. 251–252) for use with aggressive preadolescents. In this type of behavioral rehearsal instigatory situations are played out by each of the group members.

> While there are many variations of the technique, that which has proved to be the most useful requires the elicitation from the child of various situations which in the past have provoked him to aggression or defiance. These situations are then presented, through acting, in a hierarchical manner, with the mildest situation presented initially. As the child develops tolerance for these mild situations, those of a higher instigatory valence are gradually introduced. An arbitrary point score is constructed and the child's responses to instigation are rated by other group members and by the therapist. An example of such a scoring system is: Two minus points for overt expression of aggression, for example, striking out; one minus point for an 'emotional' response, for example, flushing, clenching fists, tightening of the facial musculature, and so forth. No points are given for a neutral response. On the positive side, one point is scored for a passive reaction, as for example when the child goes 'limp' when he is lifted or pushed. Finally, two points are given for a reaction involving a verbal response which in some way serves to disarm or mollify the instigator. The point system, as noted, is an arbitrary one and can doubtless be improved. However, in practice it serves to quickly differentiate for the child which behaviors are acceptable and which are not. Moreover, the points received by the child, and possibly more important, the approval he wins from the group for particularly ingenious responses, may be conceptualized as a form of social reinforcement. The procedure is one which children find enjoyable—often, of course, because (for the instigator) it serves as a way of expressing aggression, albeit a socially acceptable one. That is, the instigator is helping the other child to inhibit his own aggression, and as such is functioning in a therapeutic manner. Even the child who is provoked finds his role bearable, since it will be his turn next to play the part of the instigator. Even extremely passive children, who fear aggression, gradually find behavior rehearsal is not threatening in the context of the protective therapy setting.

Gittelman also makes implicit use of the Premack (1959) principle: high probability behavior can be used to reinforce low probability behavior. The child is rewarded for performing as the object of aggression by being the elicitor of aggression in a following rehearsal. Although one might question whether under such conditions the child might not become more comfortable in the role of elicitor of aggression, Premack reports evidence to the contrary.

Another variation of behavioral rehearsal—role instruction—utilizes the ongoing group interaction as the context of the rehearsal; that is, the new role is played while the group handles other problems meaningful to its members or performs other types of group tasks or problems. For example, Fred, who was unassertive even though he had many good ideas, was assigned to play the role of a highly participative individual for ten minutes during the regular group discussion. Hank, who annoyed people with his haranguing and sarcasm, was requested to practice reinforcing others in the group for their contributions. Prior to their performance, both roles had been spelled out in detail so that each individual could create a part compatible with his own style. At the end of the stipulated period the group members evaluated how well the actors had performed their roles, and a subsequent twenty minute practice period was assigned. The following week the actors played their roles for an entire group meeting.

Alternatively, the therapist can type out role descriptions compatible with treatment goals and distribute them early in treatment, without any discussion, to each of the members. The therapist instructs the members to play the new roles for the entire meeting and at the end of the second meeting he asks each member to develop a new role of his own choosing, following the initial model, and to hand this in at the next meeting. Each member subsequently plays his self-chosen role and in this way is helped to make a conscious selection of behavior patterns and to express it through his behavior.

Fixed role therapy, a technique similar to behavior rehearsal, has been described in great detail by Kelly (1955). The initial assessment of the patient is used to construct a fixed-role sketch of the individual. This sketch is carefully planned in terms of desirable behaviors but details are left to the "player." These are usually adaptive behaviors which are not being performed at the beginning of therapy and are frequently in marked contrast to the presenting behavioral patterns.

After an initial set of practice sessions in the therapy context, the patient is urged to "try on" the behavior in the real world and to observe the types of reactions manifested by the significant persons in his environment. The patient is encouraged in the first phase of treatment to maintain in his own mind the fiction of playing a role, the assumption being that to play "as if" reduces the threat incurred in performing new behaviors in the outside world. The environment can be explored without irrevocable commitment and because of the intentional lack of detail, the patient is free to develop his new role in ways which are comfortable to him. Fixed role therapy can be thought of as a form of behavioral rehearsal followed by a behavioral assignment to continue the rehearsal in the real world. Extending the rehearsal into the outside environment provides an additional intermediate step in the attainment and stabilization of the behavioral change goal.

In most instances children view modeling and rehearsal procedures as enjoyable diversions while they are changing their behavior. For the therapist however, modeling and rehearsal procedures are central to the whole treatment process. The reader now has information about the basic set of procedures used in the treatment of operant problems. When dealing with client anxiety, the therapist often relies on a different set of procedures; these are discussed in the following chapter.

10

Procedures for Anxiety

Therapist to members:
Now that you all are relaxed I want you to imagine that you are in the classroom and the teacher is looking in your direction. Hold the scene clearly in your mind. Now, if you are experiencing any anxiety I want you to indicate it by raising your left index finger (pauses five seconds). Good, I see that everyone is still relaxed. Now clear your mind (pause five seconds); this time I want you to imagine that the teacher is looking in your direction and apparently is about to call on you (pause). If you have any anxiety now, I want you to indicate it by raising your left index finger.

Relaxation, systematic desensitization, in vivo desensitization, emotive imagery, and covert sensitization—the procedures for altering anxiety—are overlapping techniques nearly all of which use either some form of imagery or relaxation training or both. Wolpe (1969) offers extensive discussion of these and other procedures, but here I am primarily interested in their use with the small group. (A detailed review of the research on systematic desensitization, possibly one of the most thoroughly evaluated therapeutic procedures, can be found in Paul, 1969.)

Relaxation

Relaxation, which I include as an anxiety-reducing procedure, has been avoided by many therapists because of a common belief that anxious children can not learn to relax. Yet there is evidence that not only anxious children but autistic children as well can be taught to relax if the tempo is sufficiently slow (Graziano and Kean, 1967). The most interesting finding was that in addition to a decrease of excitement response during relaxation training there was a marked decrease of generalized excitement for the remainder of the day. I have found that teaching relaxation in a group is frequently easier than teaching it individually, although the therapist must be wary of contagious giggling or horseplay. In order to avoid breakdown of the group, reinforcement should be used in shaping the relaxation procedures.

Relaxation is a skill which can be practiced in many situations; learning to relax is also a form of self-control training.

The following instructions (Rose, 1966) can be used in teaching relaxation to groups of adolescents although the language should be modified to conform to their vocabulary. All terminology should be understood before undertaking the exercise.

> Lie on the back with feet separated slightly and arms, palms up, near the body, head centered. Bring your attention into the right arm. Try to feel the muscles and then gently but deliberately tense the muscles in that arm. Slowly increase the tension until maximum tension is reached from the hand to top of the shoulder. Stretch the arm but don't lift

it, as you will then tense other muscles. Keep your attention on the arm and don't allow any other thought to enter your mind. Remain this way for five seconds. Slowly release the tension and be as aware as possible of what is happening in the arm: that the tension is leaving it, that the form of the arm is being dissolved, as it were, that only the mass remains and that it feels very heavy. Do the same with left arm. Next the right leg. Push the heel away and pull the toes toward you in order to avoid a foot cramp. Slowly increase tension until the maximum has been reached, from the foot to the thigh. Stretch the leg but do not lift it. Again, your attention is solely directed to the leg. Remain this way five seconds. Now slowly release the tension, feeling the tension leave, the form of the leg dissolve and the mass lying heavy on the ground. Do same with other leg. Now turn your attention to the pelvic girdle. To tense this area we contract the abdominal muscles and draw them slightly upwards. Then the buttocks are drawn towards one another. Forget the rest of the body, only feel the tensed area. Slowly release the muscles of abdomen and buttocks and leave the pelvic area resting heavy on the ground. Direct your attention next to the chest box. Here tense the muscles of the chest; move the shoulders towards each other from behind, tense the back and rib muscles. Proceed as above. Bring your attention to the neck. To tense it we pull the back of the head toward the nape of the neck; hold it a few seconds and slowly let it loose. Feel the difference between the tensed neck and the neck resting on the mat. Next the muscles of the face. Clench the jaws together; tense cheeks, mouth, eyelids; wrinkle the forehead. One by one release the tension in each of these. Let the muscles submit to the attraction of the earth. Let the lower jaw and cheeks feel the pull of gravity; the lips part slightly. Now start at the feet and work your way up to the head, feeling the heaviness in the different parts of the body. The feeling of heaviness is a first sign of a good relaxation. Feel the heaviness in the blood and every fiber of the body. Let the trunk sink even more . . . into the mat. Don't move anything. . . . You are completely relaxed, but you are also completely conscious and aware of the relaxation at the same time. Let the mind wander through the body to check whether anything more needs to be relaxed, if the body can sink still more into the mat. Remain this way for five minutes. After a certain time you will have the impression of floating outside your body. This is a successful relaxation. Don't jump up and run off. Slowly move your limbs and stretch and yawn. Increase the

> depth of the breathing (which becomes almost unnoticeable during the relaxing exercise), roll onto one side, stretch some more, and slowly sit up.

In addition tokens may be given in the initial phase for periods where no laughter, giggling, or horseplay occurs. Furthermore, stress is placed not on being relaxed but on giving external signs of relaxation. This impression is measured by a fellow client who ascertains the degree of relaxation (being quiet, not moving, shallow breathing, loose hands, facial expressions). If these indications are present, the client is reinforced. The buddy system can also be used in large groups; one person relaxes while another looks on. His job is to help his buddy assume the appearance of being relaxed. An excellent way to learn relaxation procedures is to teach them. Clients can become teachers after they have practiced the procedure several times with the group. Teaching can also enhance the client's status.

The therapist and other stimulus elements of treatment are gradually faded. Home assignments are monitored by a parent or older sibling but finally monitoring is stopped and the individual merely reports on his progress. (If tokens are used, they too are eliminated.) Cautela (1966) recommends frequent pairing of the relaxed state with the statement, "I am relaxed." This often enables the client to bring on the relaxed state with the verbal prompt.

The younger and the more anxious the client, the slower the pace of learning. A group of eight-year olds who were referred because of shyness and anxiety learned to control only a few muscle groups. Adolescents often find it easier to learn relaxation techniques if they are introduced by older models. One therapist took his group of adolescent girls, who were interested in Yoga and meditation, to a Yoga class where relaxation was being taught.

Systematic Desensitization

In spite of its usefulness as a set of operant behaviors and, in some cases, as a means of coping with anxiety evoking situations, there is very little evidence that relaxation alone is effective in diminishing phobias (Lomont and Edwards, 1967).

The claims of Jacobson (1938) and of Graziano and Kean (1967) for extensive cures with the relaxation procedure alone are probably due to their use of extensive training over a long period of time rather than the abbreviated training reported by Wolpe (1958). In order to treat phobias in the context of the group, his systematic desensitization is used either with one, several, or all of the group members. While the patient is relaxed (or in another state incompatible with anxiety) he is presented with an anxiety hierarchy that gradually approaches the feared object or situation.

For example, a client who was afraid to ride the bus was asked to imagine the following scenes: a picture of a bus; a bus in front of him at a bus stop; standing on the first step of a bus and stepping back off; standing in the entrance of a stopped bus; sitting in a stopped bus; sitting in a bus moving from one stop in his neighborhood to another; sitting in a bus making two stops; sitting on a bus that takes him just out of his neighborhood; sitting on a bus going downtown.

The three basic steps in desensitization, then, are: training in relaxation, development of an anxiety hierarchy, and presentation of the hierarchy. Wolpe usually begins the development of the hierarchy at about the same time he initiates relaxation training. However, the data about the anxiety stimuli are collected when the client is in his normal rather than relaxed state. It is generally collected by means of the case history, a Fear Survey Schedule (Wolpe and Lange, 1964), and additional probing into specific aspects of the data. Wolpe also uses a Willoughby questionnaire which mainly reveals anxieties in interpersonal contexts. (In order to simplify the procedure, I use questions drawn from the Willoughby without using the test itself.)

Each hierarchy is further developed by presenting the client with a number of situations which seem in some way related to his central theme. He is asked to rank these situations according to the intensity of anxiety such a situation would provoke. The therapist may rely solely on the situations which the client has actually experienced or, as Wolpe suggests, include also those which could but have never, thus far, occurred.

Quite frequently there is more than one theme of neurotic disturbance and a hierarchy is developed for each theme.

My usual approach is to record the situations on cards and have the patient rank order them. When a decision can not be made as to the higher rank of any two cards, I throw out that item which, according to the client, is less relevant. In addition the client is asked to rate each situation on a 0 to 100 scale, where 100 is absolute panic and 0 is absolute calm. Wolpe refers to this rating as the subjective unit of disturbance (SUD). It is interesting to note that patients can often make very subtle distinctions. Items which have from 5 to 10 SUD units between them are usually included in the cards. Although middle and high anxiety items are relatively easy to discover, clients often have difficulty in describing low frequency items. As a result clients are sometimes unable to take the first step successfully. In order to correct this situation, the anxiety level of middle items can be decreased by reducing the size of the phobic object, eliminating many of its characteristics, and so forth.

Once the hierarchy has been developed, relaxation and the anxiety hierarchy must be counterposed. Although there are many procedures for this (Wolpe, 1969), I report here only on the one that I use most frequently. After the client has gone through the relaxation procedures and appears to be relaxed, he is asked to indicate by raising his left index finger if he has not achieved his base line level of anxiety. (Some clients are never able to achieve total relaxation; for them twenty or even thirty SUDs may be used as the baseline.) Once the baseline has been achieved, the client is presented with an essentially neutral item (imagining he is lying on his back on a warm day and watching the clouds quietly passing overhead). If the baseline level is maintained throughout several presentations of this neutral item, the lowest item on the hierarchy is presented. Each item is repeated two to five times or until there is an indication that the anxiety is diminishing. This continues until the client has successfully experienced all of the items. If anxiety regarding any particular item is at a high level and can not be dispelled, the therapist stops work on that hierarchy. If the problem persists at the next session, he attempts to develop an intermediate item. Sometimes, however, a whole new hierarchy is discovered and must be worked with.

The number of sessions may vary from one to thirty, with the average and model group requiring approximately six to eight sessions. Their average length is forty-five minutes and the frequency ranges from daily to monthly, biweekly sessions appearing to be most common. The frequency of trials can be increased, when there are too few sessions, by taping the presentation of the hierarchies and having the client practice at home.

Group Desensitization

Systematic desensitization in groups was first described by Lazarus (1961). The hierarchy—either standardized or group development—is presented to several individuals at once. The therapist takes an upward step in the hierarchy only when all patients have successfully experienced the previous step. As a result the procedure is slower (average 20.4 sessions) than individual treatment. On the basis of an experiment in which group systematic desensitization is compared with individual systematic desensitization, but without a control group, Ihli and Garlington (1969) report that group desensitization is as effective as individual desensitization in the treatment of test anxiety. (One implication of these findings is that the group is more efficient in terms of the cost of professional time.) A number of other authors using desensitization procedures with groups of patients noted that group interaction seemed to facilitate the reduction of anxiety. Katahn, Strenger, and Cherry (1966) indicate that their patients (students) invariably reported that being able to talk to other students in the treatment context, becoming aware that others had similar problems, and learning better study habits were the crucial factors in the reduction of anxiety. Since Katahn combined desensitization and group discussion, he was not able to ascertain which variable was most significant. Lazarus (1961) noted that desensitization is facilitated by talking to persons with similar problems in a relatively nonthreatening situation.

Paul and Shannon (1966) used group discussion to develop a hierarchy list for social evaluative anxiety. At the beginning of each session the authors also provided the group with an opportunity to discuss some of the situations that provoked anxiety and to alter the hierarchies somewhat. Although the method proved significantly better than either insight therapy or a placebo, the combination of discussion and desensitization confounds the interpretation of the results. In order to deal with this Cohen (1969) compared the effects of group interaction desensitization, noninteraction desensitization, and no treatment. His instructions to the subjects in the group interaction condition follow (p. 17). "S's in this group were encouraged to discuss particular problems and alternative means of handling these problems. The discussion was directed toward issues of test anxiety and the experimenter structured discussion so that the members of the group interacted with each other. The interaction took place during the nondesensitization periods, and included discussion of intraexperimental situations (for example, the process of relaxation) as well as extraexperimental experiences (for example, performing during the actual test)." He discovered that although both types of desensitization were more effective than no treatment, group interaction plus desensitization was more effective than desensitization alone in reducing test anxiety. See also Cohen (1969), Cohen and Dean (1968), McManus (1971), Robinson and Suinn (1969), and Suinn (1968).

In a study by Kondas (1967), twenty-three sixth to eighth grade children and thirteen college students were desensitized in groups in order to reduce stage fright and examination anxiety. In this study the combination of imagination and relaxation effected significantly more change than either imagination or relaxation alone. Moreover the results remained stable five months after the end of treatment. Another noteworthy result was that systematic desensitization in groups was even more effective with children than with adult students.

In summary, it appears that group systematic desensitization is at least as effective as individual desensitization and more effective than either insight therapy, no treatment, or placebo conditions in the treatment of several types of phobias.

Relaxation and heirarchy presentation both appear to be necessary to this kind of treatment and group discussions seems to contribute to a positive outcome. In the study that involved both children and adults, results were most successful with the children.

In general, in the groups discussed in this book desensitization has been used as an auxiliary procedure to more operant techniques. Occasionally individual members have been desensitized outside the group meeting because their fears were so pronounced that they were unable to carry out the most minimal group task. In several instances subgroups of members with common fears have been desensitized as a subgroup and on one occasion within the context of the larger group. In only two cases, one of which is described below, have any therapists made use of desensitization for the whole group, although groups were never composed of members having only one type of anxiety problem, and perhaps for this reason group desensitization was not used often.

In the following example all the members were highly anxious and in most cases had many fears. They had a common fear of criticism by the teacher, although in reality they were seldom criticized. The therapist developed a hierarchy in which the following items were placed on cards.

> The teacher criticizes another child in the class.
>
> The teacher returns a paper which says, "Good but you can do better."
>
> The teacher hands back a test which says, "That's not very good, you'll have to do better."
>
> The teacher asks whether you were late when you were not late.
>
> The teacher sees you coming in late and says, "You're late; don't do it any more."
>
> The teacher tells you to turn around when you are talking to someone behind you.
>
> The teacher says firmly, "What's got into you today?"

> The teacher gets angry with you and says, "Can't you do anything right?"

The therapist developed the hierarchy by asking the group members for class situations which upset them. Because most situations involved the teacher, he simplified the hierarchy by excluding items not related to the teacher. He also did not include items which two or more members did not feel caused them any trouble. The order of items in the hierarchy was somewhat different for each member of the group.

After the members showed that they could relax for an extended period, the therapist had a session on imagination training, in which he had the children imagine different situations, beginning with ones which provoked no anxiety and occasionally including some of the situations mentioned above. After he introduced a scene he asked each child to describe what he (the child) was imagining.

At the following session the therapist put the members in a state of relaxation and presented them with the first two items. Although several members did manifest anxiety even after four or five trials, he went on to a third item. At this point they began to get restless so he terminated the practice. He asked the boys how they liked the procedure, and all reacted favorably, recommending that they continue.

At the next session the therapist decided to reinforce by marking on a group thermometer the number of minutes the group could remain relaxed, as evidenced by being quiet and still. This procedure noticeably increased the quietness of the group. He also began to chart the number of items that all the members could get through without becoming anxious. Although the charting may have inhibited them from reporting anxiety, in terms of observable physical manifestations of anxiety such inhibition did not seem to be the case. In subsequent sessions all the items were worked through. When one member could not relax or remained anxious, he was asked to stop while the others continued. If two or more persons did not relax or lose their anxiety, the desensitization session was terminated.

The entire procedure took parts of eight sessions over a period of four weeks. Usually twenty minutes of each session were devoted to it. Following the process, teachers reported that the children seemed to be less anxious in class. Most of the children reported that they were not bothered as much by the teacher's criticism.

Emotive Imagery

When relaxation does not appear to be readily learned, Lazarus and Abramovitz (1962) recommend a desensitizing procedure called emotive imagery. Instead of relaxation the therapist trains the client in anxiety-inhibiting emotive images —"images that arouse feelings of pride, mirth, the excitement of adventure, serenity or affection." Wolpe and Lazarus (1966, p. 143) offer this description of the technique:

> As in the usual method of systematic desensitization, a graduated hierarchy is drawn up. By sympathetic conversation and inquiry, the clinician establishes the nature of the child's hero images and the wish fulfillments and identifications which accompany them. The child is asked to close his eyes and imagine a sequence of events which is close enough to his everyday life to be credible, but within which is woven a story concerning his favorite hero or alter ego. When the clinician judges that these emotions have been maximally aroused, he introduces, as a natural part of the narrative, the lowest item in the hierarchy. If there is evidence that anxiety is being inhibited, the procedure is repeated as in ordinary systematic desensitization until the highest item in the hierarchy is tolerated without distress.

Although this procedure has been used on several occasions in groups, the therapists involved have reported neither the problems encountered nor the outcome in any detail. The procedure appears to be quite promising, however, and should be explored further as a technique in the treatment of anxiety responses.

Covert Sensitization

Covert sensitization was developed by Cautela (1966), who reports on its use with compulsive eating and drinking.

The compulsive behavior is paired with aversive imagery. As in systematic desensitization, the patient is taught to relax completely. While relaxed the therapist encourages the patient to imagine a situation in which eating or drinking is just beginning. At the moment of introjection the patient is asked to imagine a highly unpleasant scene (such as vomiting all over himself). The patient is told to visualize the scene once again without assistance from the therapist. When he begins to feel upset or nauseous, he indicates that to the therapist. Once again the patient is asked to visualize the eating or drinking. On this occasion the patient does not actually commit the compulsive act; feeling upset or nauseous is eliminated (through instruction), and the client remains calm and relaxed. Cautela alternates five unpleasant trials with five calm and relaxed trials.

The major prerequisite is compulsive behavior which the client is highly motivated to eliminate. The obvious purpose of the method is to attach anxiety to the compulsive act and to relieve anxiety by terminating the behavior.

Although there are only case histories to illustrate the dynamics of this procedure, the results appear most promising (see Stuart, 1967; Kolvin, 1967; Davison, 1969). To my knowledge only Kellam (1969) has reported on attempts to apply this procedure to delinquent behaviors (shoplifting) and no one has described its use with groups of clients. In my work with early juvenile offenders, however, I have used a similar procedure as a means of attaching anxiety to the delinquent act and providing anxiety relief for prosocial alternate behavior.

The clients had a history of committing delinquent acts which were usually immediately reinforcing and received postponed punishment or no punishment at all. My purpose was to create anxiety in the client when confronted with the situation in which the potentially delinquent act was possible. The group members first were confronted with the ultimate consequences or their behavior—the training school. Since verbal descriptions were ineffective, I arranged visits to the school and interviews with the pupils. (Not all training schools are aversive, especially at first glance; the therapist is advised to pick one that is.) This visit, however, would not deter them from delinquent acts for a long period of time, so it was necessary to pair the vivid and immediate (aversive) image of the institution with the delinquent act as soon after the visit to the training school as possible. This involved discussion of the salient delinquent acts, followed immediately by vivid imagery of the training school. Verbalization of the image served as an intensifier of the experience and a control on the effectiveness of the imagery. This was repeated several times during the first week and continued for several weeks.

In addition, in vivo technique was utilized. The clients were taken shopping and confronted with as many seductive embellishments as possible. At the point where the delinquent act would normally take place, the aversive image was invoked.

Even if the procedure described above is successful in pairing the delinquent act with an autonomic anxiety response, it is necessary to structure the avoidance response to obtain stable change. Although group or individual discussion of what one does when one is in a tempting situation may suffice, in most cases the therapist must present the client with a number of alternatives and train him in performing them. Providing the group with cue words—which they repeat whenever confronted with a problem situation—should recall the total aversive image and strengthen the avoidance response.

It is also important to provide a possibility for escaping the problem situation altogether. If Ed joyrides and Pete is afraid of doing this, then Ed is advised to keep Pete's company during the first period of treatment. J.J., who wants sports equipment, has to be reminded by the group to stay out of the department store and the sports shops until treatment has advanced to the point that he can handle temptation. In addition, of course, an entirely new battery of socially acceptable behaviors has to be built up, requiring a variety of procedures and individual plans for each client.

At this point there is only anecdotal or case evidence to support the use of this procedure. Because it is usually used in conjunction with other procedures, interpretation of its contribution is impossible. But especially in the absence of sufficient procedures for reduction of delinquent acts, it appears to be worth further exploration.

It is clear from this chapter that not all anxiety is maladaptive and that procedures are available for both decreasing and increasing anxiety. These procedures along with those discussed in the previous four chapters provide the basic armamentarium of the behavioral therapist. In addition to using these procedures to attain individual treatment goals, the group therapist has the additional advantage of utilizing the group task as well as various group structures. In the next chapter the nature of the group task and its relation to treatment goals are discussed.

11

Group Task

Friend: *What do you do in that group?*
Clients: *We play games like Scrabble, pool, and concentration. We have quizzes and spelling contests where we can win prizes. We're making a clubhouse with a bird feeder, a bookcase, and a huge mural. We go to the museums and to the zoo. We get lessons in basketball and play real games. We earn salaries for doing homework and get to spend our money in a neat store. And we talk about all kinds of things.*

Every group has work to accomplish in common. Members of the therapy groups must learn to work together to attain group and individual goals. Their tasks may be recreational, academic, or vocational. Regardless of their nature, however, all tasks must facilitate the attainment of treatment and group goals. Vinter's definition of group program (1967b, p. 95) is especially useful: "A general class of group activities, each of which consists of an interconnected, sequential series of social behaviors. They are usually infused with and guided by meanings and performance standards from the larger culture. The social behaviors which constitute any particular activity tend to follow a more-or-less typical pattern, unfolding in a rough chronological sequence, and, for some, reaching a definite climax or conclusion."

Individual tasks do not fall within this definition even though they are, of course, valuable experience for the clients. Similarly there are instructional and unplanned interactive activities, which, though essential for good group functioning, are not, in the sense meant here, group tasks. The word *task* rather than *program* is used because of the broad meaning commonly given to the latter in social-work literature—namely, everything that occurs from the beginning to the end of a group meeting—whereas *task* implies only a job to be done.

The purpose of this chapter is to develop criteria for the selection of group tasks appropriate to the attainment of specific group and individual treatment goals. To this end I discuss a set of concepts and describe a number of examples of the relationship of group tasks to treatment goals. The concepts derive primarily from the work of Vinter (1967a), who in turn borrowed and extended the ideas of Gump and Sutton-Smith (1955).

Every task has several overlapping components. The first is the physical field—the material attributes which make the task possible and the types of space arrangement required for performance. The second is the rules or prescriptions as to how the materials are to be used and how the quality of the outcome is to be judged. The third is the behavior actually performed by the participants. The behavior is basically of two sorts: that which is required by the prescriptions and that which, though regulated by custom, is neither formally prescribed nor necessary. These are referred to, respectively, as prescribed and informal behavior (Vinter's constituent and respondent activities). The fourth component is the contingencies associated with appropriate performances or the attainment of certain prescribed goals. The therapist has at his disposal the manipulation of the materials, the establishment of the prescriptions, and the management of the contingencies, all in the service of behavioral change. Thus, the task is a crucial tool in the treatment of children in groups. In this chapter, I shall analyze some of these characteristics as they impinge on the behavior of the participants.

Prescriptions For Task Behavior

The activities associated with all group tasks vary in the degree of prescription. In some tasks (such as tournament chess) virtually all activities, including the behavior of the onlookers, are prescribed. In games without names, in which children merely alternate who chases whom, few if any prescriptions exist. Since our clients differ radically in their initial capacity to handle prescriptions of any sort, the degree of prescriptiveness is highly pertinent to group task planning and selection. For the clients who find it difficult to submit to the control of rules, tasks with few prescriptions are selected initially. Since behavior is also readily controlled by its consequences, more attention is given to rewards than to rules, at first, as a means of control. A similar plan is followed for those clients who are subjected to highly prescribed home or school situations and are unable as a result to make decisions for themselves. In addition, these clients are encouraged and trained to develop their own prescriptions.

The intensity of interaction will vary according to task prescriptions and a further distinction is made between permitted and required intensity. Many children will or can learn to respond when interaction is possible but not obligatory; for other children the opposite is true. Activities are chosen which take into consideration the children's requirements for the degree of permitted and required interaction. A high degree of interaction would not be attempted initially in a group of withdrawn or anxious children. Parallel play activities might be encouraged, and as members come in contact with each other on their own, new rules or new games would increase the degree of interaction gradually. As the children exhibit diminished overt anxiety manifestations with one another, subgroup games may be introduced. Eventually noncompetitive group activities requiring structured verbal or motoric contributions would be encouraged, and finally competitive play could be introduced.

Because control is a major problem for many clients, prescribed behavior must be considered in terms of who prescribes the behavior. If a group of delinquents refuses to accept adult prescriptions, tasks must be developed which are characterized by prescriptions inherent in the task. If a few group members tyrannize the others, activities should be selected in which peers prescribe behavior for each other more equally. Where anxious clients predominate, prescriptions may be initially therapist imposed and gradually withdrawn.

Types of Task Behavior

Inherent in the group task may be prescriptions for either cognitive, motoric, or affective behaviors. The therapist must select those tasks which provide the client with practice in the behavioral area in which the client is deficient.

For children who have difficulty expressing their feelings, tasks must be developed which encourage affective responses. Drama, role-playing, aggressive games, and sensitivity-training sessions tend to provide prompts for the expression of a wide variety of feelings and reduce the emphasis on cognitive and motoric responses. The affectively flat or inappropriate child is an exception, however; task planning should usually focus on creating conditions which will develop cognitive and motoric skills and those behavioral controls absent from the clients repertoire.

The therapist's selection of a task must obviously take into consideration the skill level of the members in relation to it. A problem-solving discussion in which there are rules that only one person at a time may speak and that one must raise one's hand and be recognized by the chairman would drastically curtail participation or encourage rule-breaking among many groups of predelinquents in the first phase of treatment. Since it is often the aim of the therapist to broaden motoric skills in areas which will relate the clients eventually to their immediate subculture, skill training may be introduced first, in order to attain the skill level which will make the activity rewarding. Because skill training in itself is relatively unrewarding, tokens may be given to the members until, having developed the necessary skill, the reinforcement inherent in the activity increases and overt reinforcement is withdrawn.

Task Contingency Structure

The therapist initially provides activities which are abundant in rewards or, if they are not inherently available in the activity, the therapist provides external rewards. As the clients learn to delay their gratification, they can move on to activities with fewer immediate rewards. When the members claim that a game is fun, exciting, or interesting, one can usually assume that it has certain reinforcement value. A frequently-chosen activity may be utilized by the therapist as reinforcement for one less frequently chosen. For example, when the therapist attempted to develop a program in which homework skills could be taught and homework actually performed, there was considerable opposition. However, when the therapist made available a highly popular street game, on the provision that equal time would be given to "school-playing," a struggle was avoided.

Rewards are not the only contingencies attached to tasks since aversive stimuli often follow as well. For example, in highly competitive sports one side must lose. For this reason we speak of a "contingency structure" rather than a reward structure (cf. Vinter). In many activities the aversive contingencies are a major source of control; prescriptions are maintained because deviants are punished by their peers or the referees. A careful analysis of the contingency structure of a group task will consider both reinforcement and punishment related to prescriptive behaviors in order to determine whether the task will meet client needs.

The reinforcement potential of most activities can be increased if tokens are distributed for the achievement of predetermined standards such as cooperative behavior and good sportsmanship. Early in treatment, reinforcement may be contingent merely on looking as if one is playing. As treatment progresses the rewards inherent in the activity are increasingly stressed.

The status of a given activity in the extra-group play environment often determines its reward value in the treatment group. It is sometimes useful, therefore, to provide group members with the minimal skills necessary to participate in the normative sociorecreational activities of their community. Accordingly, repetitive but relatively uncreative activities may be encouraged (stickball, and so on) and even trained for.

Categories of Group Tasks

The therapist must also decide such questions as the length, number, and types of tasks in each phase of treatment. In the initial phase, especially with children twelve or younger, varied activities lasting only ten to fifteen minutes each are used. This enables the therapist to provide the stimulus conditions for many types of desired behavior and at the same time increases the frequency of possibilities for reinforcement. It also takes into account the limited attention span of most young clients. As treatment progresses, the activity periods will become longer for older children.

Three or four activities can be included in the typical meeting (forty-five minutes to an hour and a half) and usually include at least one school-simulated activity, training in and/or participation in one athletic activity or sport, one table game, and a group discussion, the only invariable task. Alternate tasks often included are role-plays, communication games, and, if a token-economy is in operation, a trip to the "store." The simulated school activity is included because most clients have difficulty in adapting to school norms. In order to create interest in these activities, they are usually heavily rewarded in the first phase of treatment. As the members perceive the results of improvement in school, the teacher's praise is usually sufficient to sustain the behavior. During the simulated schoolroom activities, the therapist assumes much of the teacher's role and as meetings progress he becomes stricter, demands more attention, and in general tries to recreate the classroom atmosphere. The purpose usually is to train the client in the classroom skills he needs to learn academic skills.

Delinquents and withdrawn and anxious clients not only lack the skills for adapting to classroom demands, but most also lack sports and other physical recreation skills. For this reason, a physical activity is also usually included in each meeting, and the therapist normally spends part of the time devoted to this activity in training the members in performance skills.

As noted earlier intensive preparation often yields too few rewards. As a result it becomes important for members to participate in the athletic activity under conditions similar to those on the playground. At first members play against each other or against other treatment groups. Later they may be able to play other street or community center teams. Another set of athletic activities often taught in group treatment is wrestling, boxing, and judo, all of which are especially useful to children who are frequently physically abused in their neighborhood.

Table games, too, can help develop useful skills, especially when they are related to academic activities. Different games provide varying degrees of interaction and the therapist will use them accordingly. Games may also be encouraged in the later phase of treatment as a means of relating the client's skills to the interests of his other friends or family. Of course, the therapist can devise endless "games" to encourage communication skills and other desired behaviors.

Group discussion is an activity common to virtually all group meetings. Most clients have difficulty with such skills as decision-making in groups, discussing an idea systematically, or disagreeing (without getting angry) with another, despite the fact that they may have adequate intellectual capacities. Group discussion also keeps the focus on treatment goals; if there are too many recreational activities, members often lose sight of the group's therapeutic purposes. Group discussion is also the time for analysis and determination of behavioral assignments, treatment contract revision, general planning, and assessment of communicative strengths and problems.

The uses of role-play and skits have been discussed.

These activities are more central to the treatment of older children, but even in groups of six- to seven-year-olds, they may sometimes be successfully used to practice creativity and spontaneity. Handcrafts and drawing are often used as a means of increasing manual dexterity and spontaneity. For many clients these may be highly aversive early in treatment and should be avoided. For others, they may be preferred activities because they provide a safe means for avoiding interaction. These tasks can move from a low to high degree of interaction by changing from individual to group projects. Moreover, they can provide a means of relating the members to the community in the later phases of treatment if an exhibition is arranged for parents and friends. Field trips provide occasions for practicing in the real world some of the social skills learned in the group and also give clients an opportunity to develop planning and organization skills.

Stimulating New Interests

Although I have suggested a variety of activities in which group members can participate, most clients are characterized by an extremely limited repertoire of social-recreational skills and interests and their history of failure in attempting new tasks tends to discourage any exploration of new possibilities. For this reason, it is often necessary for the therapist to plan not only the activities but also the means of stimulating interest in them. The major procedure for stimulating interest is the use of tokens.

Another procedure, however, long used by the recreational specialists but seldom by therapists, is the use of a "program table." The props needed in group activities are placed on the table with books, articles, or pictures illustrating a particular activity in more detail. The therapist is responsible for keeping the table full at first, but as members gain skill and interest, they are encouraged to add properties and pictures of their own. Similar to this approach is planned observation of an activity on television. Modeling procedures and behavior rehearsal are also used to stimulate interest in and reduce anxiety about new programs.

A Case in Point

In order to give the reader a picture of how group tasks are used in coordination with reinforcement and other procedures, as well as the response of children to these tasks, a detailed account of an early group meeting is presented below.

Ron, Paul, and Marv, ten, had been referred to the agency by the school. All had difficulty attending to the teacher, listening to peers, staying in their seats, and following instructions. When the therapist got to the room, he asked the boys to sit at the table while he set up the store. The boys sat down but soon came over to the store and expressed delight with what they saw. They discussed the price tags on each item and began to imagine how they would spend their chips. When the store was completed, the therapist again asked the boys to be seated. He took out the envelopes of chips and again explained how they could be used to buy models. There was a new envelope with Marv's name on it; giving it to Marv, he said, "You weren't here last week when we started. Last week each boy got three chips for coming. This week each of you will get one chip for coming and you, Marv, will get three more so you can start with the other boys. The boys also got a candy bar for coming last week, so you get one too."

The therapist then explained, "The first game we are going to play is concentration. There are two rules you have to follow to earn the chips: you must stay in your seat—that means you have to have all your weight on the chair—and you must wait until the person before you turns his two cards back. If you follow the rules for ten minutes you will earn one chip. If all three of you follow the rules, each of you will get one bonus chip." Ron and Marv each earned a chip but Paul didn't because he didn't wait until Marv had turned his two cards over. The therapist noticed that Ron went out of turn quite often.

The second game was Red Light, Green Light. Before the therapist started the game he said, "You guys have been calling each other names like 'dirty rat' and 'Frankenstein.' If each of you can go for three minutes without calling anyone a name, including those two names, each of you will get a chip. If one of you calls someone a name, you won't get a chip, but the others will. There is no bonus this time." Marv asked "How about 'rat fink'?" The therapist replied, "Yes, that counts as a name." The boys played for two minutes after which Paul stopped playing and just waited for the time to runout. No name calling occurred and all the boys got one chip. The boys again played the game fairly and Ron offered Marv his turn in front: "Take my turn, you haven't been up front yet."

The longest activity was the writing exercise. The therapist showed the boys a picture (boat, men, ocean) and put it on the table in front of them. "This is going to be a writing exercise. I want each of you to write a two-part essay. In the first part, write down what you see in this picture. In the second part, write a story about what you see. Make up anything you want to. There is only one rule this time. You must stay in your seat the whole twenty minutes. Each person who stays in his seat the whole time gets four chips." The boys asked several questions about the writing, but all stayed in their seats and all got four chips. After this was completed, the therapist said that each would have a chance to earn one more chip if they would listen quietly while each person read his story. While this was intended to reward listening behaviors, it also rewarded standing up and reading in front of others. Marv said he wouldn't read his, but when it was his turn, he did so, even though his grammar and presentation were poor. After all the stories were read and each had earned a chip, the therapist said that each boy should take a small piece of paper and write down which story was best. The one with the most votes would get one more chip. Paul won the chip.

Clay was put out on the table and the boys were told that if they stayed in their seats and did not throw any clay they would each receive three chips. The behaviors were interdependent since one had to make a house, one a car, and one a fence around both. Toward the end of the ten minutes Ron and Marv jumped out of their seats to get pencils to work in more detail and Paul was the only one who got three chips.

The next activity was the arithmetic exercises the therapist had prepared. This apparently created an unpleasant situation for Marv, who was extremely weak in arithmetic. Whereas Paul completed most of the problems and Ron about half, Marv finished only two. There had been two rules—remaining in seat and raising one's hand before talking (whispering to self was allowed). This was a fifteen-minute exercise during which the boys were to do their best without losing chips if the answers were wrong. Before they started Ron said, "Yeah, you don't lose chips for getting them wrong, but you have to work on them real hard." During the period Marv quit doing the problems and stared at the models on the table across the room. He then looked at his pile of chips and with obvious effort picked up his pencil and began working again. At the end of the period Paul spoke without raising his hand but the other two boys got four chips. The therapist did not grade the papers or make any comparisons.

Toward the end of the meeting the boys were at the store discussing how many chips were needed for each item. They were reminded that the store wouldn't be open until the meeting was over and asked which of the previous activities they would like to do again in the last ten minutes. Concentration was their choice but they all asked to receive as many chips as possible this time. The game was played for ten minutes with the same rules but if they were followed each boy was awarded five chips and one bonus. Although Paul went out of turn, the other two received their chips. At the close of the meeting Ron and Paul had twenty chips and Marv had twenty-four. Ron traded his for a plane but both of the others asked that their chips be saved for the large models.

All of the procedures which have been discussed thus far have been oriented toward modifying the behavior of individuals within the group. As the reader may have observed in the foregoing discussion, group task is a more general and complicated procedure than any thus far discussed and encompasses all of the others. In addition to the tasks having a contingency structure, other procedures such as rehearsal, modeling, and desensitization may be built into the tasks. Why then, the reader may ask, use the concept? For the group member, what he does in the group, his work and play, is the most important aspect. When asked to describe the group, he will usually describe its tasks. When asked why he is attracted to the group, he will often reply: "Because of the group task." However, there are other bases of attraction to the group. These will be discussed in the following chapter.

12

Increasing Group Attraction

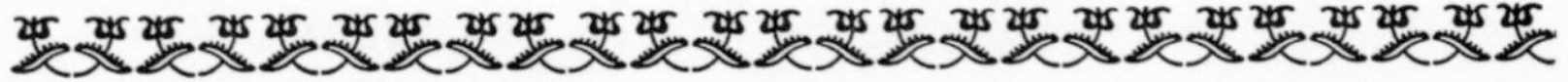

The four boys had already been waiting for ten minutes when the therapist let them in. Their eyes fell immediately on the table of food. "What's that for?" cried out Gene. "Just for coming," the therapist replied. After the boys noisily filled themselves with chocolate cake and pop, their attention turned to the model airplanes. "Can we play with these?" "Sure," responded the therapist. "And you can keep them if you earn enough tokens." The boys clamored for information on how they could get tokens. As the therapist was explaining, the group aide, a high school basketball player, rushed into the room and shot a ball at the therapist, who in turn began passing it around to the others. When the therapist finally announced that it was time to get ready to leave, several of the boys responded, "Do we gotta go already?"

The four boys slouched in their chairs, waiting for something to happen. After the therapist explained the purpose of the group, he asked whether there were any questions. "Yeah," said Tommy. "When do we go home?" The boys wandered through the room looking at the toys, tools, and games. When the therapist suggested a game they could play together, Anthony said that he didn't want to play.

When individuals have reinforcing properties for each other, they are more likely to cluster together since association is intermittently reinforced (Staats and Staats, 1963). When individuals have aversive properties for each other, avoidance behaviors would be negatively reinforced by the termination of the aversive stimulation. If activities are continuously reinforcing, the individuals paired with those activities become conditioned positive reinforcers. If the activities are aversive, the opposite is likely. This clustering effect may be referred to as group attraction or cohesiveness. Thibaut and Kelley (1959) analyze group cohesiveness in terms of the rewards and costs to an individual where he belongs to the group: the greater the rewards in proportion to the costs, the higher the attraction. They also point out that as long as the expected reward-cost ratio (or outcome) is better than that offered by the client's best alternative environment, he will remain in the group. The gang-member client usually has highly valued alternatives with which the therapist's reinforcers must compete. For a child with home and school behavior problems, however, few if any alternatives exist. On the other hand, most of their previous group experiences have been highly aversive.

According to many writers on the subject (see especially Cartwright, 1968), attraction to the group may be based on the attractiveness of its members, the group activities, or its status in the eyes of significant nongroup members. The attractiveness of the therapist and the effectiveness of the group in reducing the initial anxiety characteristic of most new situations also may be contributing factors (Goldstein, 1966).

Pros and Cons

In most types of group treatment the therapist is concerned with increasing the attractiveness of the group for its members, at least during the early and middle phases of group treatment. There are several advantages to the highly attractive group: one can expect its members to attend regularly; there is greater likelihood of member conformance to group norms; its reinforcers will be more potent and of wider variety; there is greater likelihood of imitation of its models, provided prosocial models are available (Cartwright, 1968).

However, high group attraction is a two-edged sword. If the group is too attractive, members may spend most of their energy maintaining it and reinforcing each others' minimal accomplishments. Activities which gain the group's recognition become more highly valued than increasing needed social skills. To the degree that no other social situation provides satisfaction, this state of extremely high attractiveness hinders the attainment of treatment goals. The group as a whole may avoid tasks which detract from a desirable state of affairs; they may find it difficult to give up the group when they have achieved treatment goals or when the treatment period is over. Finally, if a group is attractive but its norms are antitherapeutic, its advantages work against the goals of increasing prosocial and decreasing antisocial behaviors. The gang is an excellent example of a highly attractive group with antitherapeutic norms. In most cases the street worker would be ill-advised to increase its attractiveness and in practice, as might be expected, its members are encouraged to find nongang associates and activities which eventually will lower the attractiveness of the group.

Reinforcing Attendance

Continuance in group treatment is a major concern. Some clients will remain in treatment during the early phase even if the group appears unattractive. If this perception is unchanged in later phases, the client will drop out, attend irregularly, or continue but will probably not accept the therapeutic norms of the group. If the client does not find the group itself initially rewarding—and this is often the case—the therapist can increase its attraction by providing reinforcement for attendance and offering rewards to the entire group for performance of desired behaviors.

Promoting Positive Evaluative Statements

In many children's groups, however, rewards based on group achievement in the initial phase of treatment may be ineffectual since clients may be afraid to risk failure caused by someone else. Using only simple reinforcement procedures—a signal light indicating psychological insight—Oakes (1962) was successful in increasing a verbal response class of "giving opinion." Similar results have been demonstrated by Hastorf (1965) and Bavelas, Hastorf, Gross, and Kite (1968).

Verbal reinforcement of all positive evaluative statements about persons in the group, the usefulness of the group, group activities, and so on, results in an increase in the frequency of such statements and greater attraction to the group. Similarly, most therapists, at least early in treatment, tend to extinguish negative evaluative statements.

The question may be raised whether one thereby causes the clients to repress negative feelings. Expressed frequently enough, however, the statements a person makes tend to become the "real" description of what he perceives to be his actual emotional state; a statement of liking seems to lead to a state of liking. It is only rarely that such a concomitant change does not occur. When it does not, therapists have found it useful to use the familiar psychodynamic technique of identifying the negative feelings about the group and encouraging members to express them. This appears to be useful only if it is followed by a task-oriented revision of the specific procedures which seem to be annoying members; that is, encouragement of negative statements should lead to an evaluation of on-going practices and to a possible change in them. There is a tendency for psychodynamically-oriented group therapists to assume that underlying all group process is a basic or inherent hostility which must be unrepressed. As a result, one can observe that the large proportion of verbal statements in such groups are of an angry and hostile nature. This occurs not because of the nature of all groups or clients but because such statements are reinforced. It is my experience that in most (but not all) groups, nonspecific negative statements need not be encouraged and in no group is it necessary to hold a discussion of primarily negative conditions more than once or twice in the series of sessions. Of course, if there is an absence of positive evaluative statements regarding the group, it may be necessary to provide models to demonstrate them and, hopefully, to evoke similar statements from the others.

Providing Attractive Tasks

Once the members have arrived and have been reinforced for attendance, they need to be motivated to remain. The major focus is on developing activities in which the clients enjoy participating. In terms of increasing attraction to the group, it is useful to provide activities initially which are not available elsewhere, which are compatible with subcultural taste patterns, and which are within the immediate skill level of the participants.

The cash basis for trying out treatment may be an inexpensive way of involving adolescents (Schwitzgebel, 1967). The drop-out rate appears to be much lower and the time between initial contact and work on a meaningful treatment plan shorter than other known methods with highly resistive clients. (Reduced costs in therapist time even out the client "salaries.") Salaries also reduce the stigma attached to treatment groups because the clients' relationship is strictly contractual. Their work, for which they are earning a salary, is to try out new behaviors eventually. It is not a deceptive approach, as some critics suggest, insofar as the purposes of the salary are stipulated in advance. Initially, clients are motivated solely by financial gain or the possibility of "conning the straights." Eventually, other less tangible rewards keep them in treatment.

Reducing Initial Anxiety

Attendance at a group meeting with strange children, strange adults, demands not yet comprehended, and a strange physical environment drive many children to a state of near panic. It is no wonder that many children do not make it to a first meeting. Several approaches may overcome this initial anxiety: it is helpful to meet in a familiar place; if possible, each should come with a friend (it is not necessary for the friend to continue in the group); the therapist should become familiar to the client prior to the first meeting; the therapist should describe during the intake interview where the group will meet, what the other children are like, what the activities will be during the first meeting, and what rewards are available. He may use a tape recording, a film, or video tape of a typical initial meeting. The therapist also may want to consider the possibility of providing transportation; some anxious children will find this reassuring and it will help to overcome their initial inertia.

Once the clients arrive, they can be driven away by anxiety-eliciting activities. In general, the therapist holds demands to a minimum at the first meeting: he uses positive reinforcing procedures; he protects members from attack by each other; he introduces tasks which are familiar and attractive. Even broad interaction is not too strongly encouraged, especially for clients with a high degree of interpersonal anxiety. Parallel play is structured with most interaction occurring in subgroups or between therapist and client. One should avoid, however, eliminating all discussion of treatment goals and contract in the attempt to reduce anxiety. Otherwise the group is seen as a purely recreational group, and it is difficult to overcome this initial stereotype.

Punishing for Discontinuance

Attendance at out-patient treatment sessions is occasionally designed as a legal alternative to institutionalization in a juvenile home or house of correction. If attendance does not occur, the therapist may be hesitant to use this powerful contingency and to the extent that the client is aware of this reticence, he will probably avoid the sessions. If the therapist is going to show his wares to a highly resistive client, the minimal attendance requirement should be rigidly adhered to at least for the first several sessions. Once the client is present, of course, his voluntary participation can be shaped and his motivation increased.

If it is possible, as suggested earlier, the therapist should try to reduce pressure by meeting these clients in their own neighborhood. He can also point out that although attendance is required, the client need not say anything. His job is only to collect enough information to decide whether he wishes to continue. If highly attractive activities are made available (filming, pool, motorcycle rides), my experience confirms that most clients will stay well beyond the period required by the juvenile authorities.

Another way to increase continuance is the requirement of a deposit, refunded only if the client completes the attendance requirements for the first or all phases of the group's duration. Small amounts can be returned as the client completes other contractual requirements. This is not effective with highly resistive clients but for those who are actively seeking help and who have some initial concern, a deposit appears to be extremely useful. There does not appear to be any financial level below which the deposit cannot be used; one merely adjusts the size of the deposit to fit (uncomfortably) the specific budget. My experience with the use of deposits has been with parents' groups and groups of students who wanted to stop smoking, lose weight, or improve study habits. In all these cases, more than 85 per cent of the members continued to the end of treatment (Rose and others, 1970).

Increasing Interaction

Homans (1961) notes that in most cases increased interaction results in increased attraction and that in time each member becomes a conditioned positive reinforcer for the others except when the interaction is primarily aversive. One way for the interaction to become aversive is to limit the number of reinforcers available to the group, which results in competition among members for these limited but valued resources and consequently to a lowering of group attraction.

Following Homan's suggestions, early in treatment (but not at the first meeting for highly anxious clients) broad participation is encouraged. Nonparticipants or inactive participants are reinforced for verbal contributions. They are trained prior to the meeting in responses they can make and are prompted to make them. In general, shaping is used to move from brief and irrelevant comments to extensive and highly relevant (as determined by the group norms) comments. If the new skills in participation are to be maintained, natural reinforcement in the form of response by others is necessary. Initially, group members may be reinforced for responding regardless of relevance. Later, however, as the passive members acquire courage and skill, the therapist allows the natural reinforcement process to occur in order to promote discrimination training. He may have to protect the passive client from too great an arbitrariness on the part of his peers through the use of intermittent reinforcement for contributions not recognized by the other members.

Some members' verbal contributions to group interaction exclude the possibility of participation by less forceful members. This behavior is not only maladaptive in the context of the treatment group but may be a general problem in all social groups to which the domineering client belongs. In order to decrease the almost inevitable aversiveness of such an individual and consequently to increase the participation of others and the attractiveness of the group, an interesting procedure using stopwatches has been developed (see Chapter Thirteen) in which each member attempts to participate as near to the average group time as possible.

Providing External Pressure

Related to Homans' work are the investigations of Sherif and Sherif (1953); Myers (1962); and Julian, Bishop, and Fiedler (1966) which conclude that intergroup competition results in increased group attractiveness; that is, a common (implied) threat draws the members together and offers an opportunity for increased interaction. If intergroup competition is to be used to increase the attractiveness of the group in treatment the group should have an opportunity to reap at least limited rewards from the experience and the group should be aware that its cooperative endeavor is a means of obtaining these rewards or resolving the implied threat.

Similar to competition in its effect on cohesiveness is a group performance or demonstration for a larger audience. Most of the clients with whom I have worked have seldom if ever participated in this kind of experience prior to treatment. One group put on a skit for their school and another collected old clothes from their schoolmates to give to the Salvation Army. One therapist took his group to eat in a restaurant. Although he used this as a group reward, it also represented a self-imposed external threat. Another group invited the board of directors of the agency (which included a judge and a city councilman) to a group meeting. Such ventures place members back in what has previously been considered a threatening community but the existence of the group serves to attenuate members' fears. If these projects occur relatively late in the group's history, clients will be able to handle the threat without feeling impelled to leave the group. When groups choose their own projects, moreover, the threat is self-imposed.

The extensive preparation required for the success of such projects creates a high level of interaction which in turn tends to reduce the anxiety associated with the new venture. Covert behavioral rehearsal can be used to desensitize the more anxious members.

In summary, if a group is to be placed in a situation that they perceive as an external threat, they should decide for themselves to make that step and should either have or be taught the skills to cope with it. In most cases, threat procedures should not be used until the middle phase of treatment. If the group members are led to view themselves as an attractive group or led to expect that they will become an attractive group, the probability is high that they will eventually describe themselves in those terms. Therapists using this approach are advised to assure members of the unusual compatibility of the members and the high probability of becoming an attractive group. In fact, this is an accurate and fair portrayal of almost all groups in which the therapist attempts to increase cohesiveness: the members do eventually become compatible; they do become highly attractive to the group.

But high attraction is not the only group goal. Ways of using behavioral procedures for attaining other group goals are explained in the following chapter.

13

Group Structures

There appeared to be an unwritten law in the group that if a member complained about anything the others would tease him. After a while, nobody complained any more.

Harry and Allan were always off in a corner doing something together. Jack and Jimmy stayed close to the therapist, while Cabot always played by himself.

Group structure refers to the set of relatively stable attributes in terms of which the group can be analyzed or described. These structures include patterns of interpersonal liking (subgroup structure); patterns of informal rules (norm structure) patterns in which group members communicate (communication structure); and the distribution of leadership functions (leadership structure). Some forms of each of these structures tend to facilitate attainment of treatment goals; others tend to hinder it. Although some treatment procedures modify individual behavior, others are oriented primarily toward modifying group structures, group processes (the patterns by which structures change), or the degree of group attractiveness. In group treatment both types of modifications are usually worked out at the same time. Helping Johnny to become more assertive in the group may be an effective way to develop a more equal pattern of group communication. Limiting Fred so that he no longer does all the work and makes all the decisions results in a change in his pattern of responses as well as a new distribution of group leadership functions. In this chapter I discuss those indirect means of intervention which establish or modify group norms, status structure, leadership structure, patterns of communication, and subgroup structure.

Group Norms

Homans (1961, p. 46) defines a norm as "a statement made by a number of members of the group, not necessarily all of them, that the members ought to behave in a certain way in certain circumstances." Even when this statement is not explicit, the norm may still be implied from the consistency of members' behavior. The norm functions as discriminative stimulus for behavior. Members learn it when they perceive that deviations are punished by group pressures or sanctions in various forms and that conformity is rewarded at least intermittently by approval. The potency of the norm seems to be related to the frequency and regularity of such reward and punishment.

In working with a group the therapist establishes many rules prescribing what behaviors are permitted, obligatory, and so on. If members adhere to these prescriptions, they function as norms. Group members also however bring norms with them from other settings. Established norms in a given group are those for which conformance is reinforced and nonconformance extinguished or punished. Since the therapist controls powerful reinforcers in the initial phase of treatment, he is in a position to establish his rules as the major norms. However, when working with natural or well-established groups, the therapist confronts norms which have a long history of reinforcement, and his attempts to establish new ones are weakened.

Examples of group norms, many of which have been

discussed in previous chapters, include (1) members should not interrupt one another; (2) members should help each other to solve problems; (3) members, when asked in the group, should be able to talk about their behavioral problems; (4) when discussing his problems, a member should take some responsibility for their occurrence; (5) "when a fellow member does something that helps the group, let him know!"; (6) members should attend meetings regularly.

In the following example the therapist uses prompting as the major means of modifying the group norm. Before she used this procedure, she confronted the members with the problem, involved them in finding a group goal and procedures for attaining it, used modeling and rehearsal to train them in prompting, and reinforced them for conforming to the agreed upon plan. Thus, a series of procedures was required to establish a new norm.

The group members had a tendency to stray from the topic under discussion, frequently jumping from one topic to another. They become involved in discussions that were irrelevant and unrelated to the problem-solving goals of the group. Members reinforced each other by quickly becoming involved in these casual conversations. The desired norm was that members stay with a discussion until they had "solved" the problem or come up with suggestions for dealing with it. This norm would facilitate attainment of the treatment goals. Although none of the procedures discussed here are new to the reader, this example puts them together in a novel way to describe what a group norm is.

The techniques employed by the therapist were as follows: she stated the nature of the problem and the rationale for desiring a new norm to make the members aware of the need for the norm and thereby to attain support from them for introducing it. The therapist asked for suggestions on how the group could adapt to the new norm in order to involve the members in the change process; by making change an agreed upon group goal, the therapist hoped to create group pressures to conform. The therapist then adopted the group's suggestion of reminding one another as a procedure and established the policy that each member employ the phrase, "We were discussing ———————" when she recognized straying from the topic. Here the therapist established the group members rather than herself as agents of norm modification since the members had been reinforcing each other's dysfunctional behavior. She next suggested that the members immediately put the new procedure into effect for the remainder of the meeting and added that she too would employ the specified phrase under the discussed condition. She then served as a model for the behavior expected of the members. When a member recognized another girl inappropriately changing the topic, she used the new technique. The therapist nonverbally rewarded her by smiling and nodding approval. For the remainder of the meeting (about ten minutes), the girls adhered to the new rule of sticking to the topic. At the end of the meeting the therapist pointed to the members' use of the phrase and praised the group for its adherence to the suggested norm and new technique. At the next meeting the therapist reminded the group of the new technique. She found it necessary to employ it herself and did so. Several members used it also, resulting in a decrease in abrupt and irrelevant topic changing.

In this example, the therapist attempted to delimit deviation from the norm. But not all deviant behavior can or should be eliminated. In such cases deviation serves the important function of facilitating a revision of the group structure. Norms which may have once been useful may later lose their utility. The deviant, in his successful attempts, challenges the norm, and his challenge may result in a reexamination of the norm by the group. The deviant who challenges all norms, however, evokes aversive responses to his actions and person, and his deviant behavior may be the target of treatment. In its mildest form this treatment frequently involves a simple group extinction procedure. In other situations a role instruction method may be used: the deviant is instructed to play the role of conformer, and group members are instructed to reinforce him by giving attention to all acts of conformance in previously deviant areas. Behavioral assignments may be used for the child who is deviant in school.

Status Structure

Homans (1961) views the status of an individual in terms of the other members' evaluations of his prestige or importance within the group. That prestige may be based on his ability to perform highly valued behaviors or to control valued resources. It may also be in part a function of his status in other groups or in the larger community. In one school referral group the person of highest status was the one who talked back to the teacher the most. In another group it was the one who could fight best on the playground. The lowest status persons in both groups were those who were regarded by their peers as sissies because of a lack of assertive responses in relation to peers or authority figures.

High status brings rewards. Hollander (1960) found that one of the fruits of high status is protection from punishment (loss of status) for deviation. He calls this reward idiosyncrasy credit. No such credit is available to the low status member. Wiggins, Dill, and Schwartz (1968) found that high status compared with middle status persons are punished less for minor deviations but more for major ones. Although Wiggins presents no data on low status persons, one can extrapolate from these findings that they would be punished for still smaller deviations. That verbal aggression toward a person seems to increase as his status decreases is the conclusion drawn by Worchel (1957) as the result of laboratory studies on frustration-aggression.

Low status in treatment groups usually belongs to children who suffer the indignity of such status in all the groups to which they belong. For these children group experience provides not only a minimum of positive reinforcement such as praise from peers, encouragement, shared goods or activities, and friendly remarks but also powerful aversive stimulation. They are the objects of scapegoating and aggressive behavior by peers. They are blamed for all the group's misfortunes; they are teased, pushed, hit, and snubbed whenever the person in authority turns his back. They are poorly integrated into the group structure. (See, especially, Feldman, 1969, who describes the position of the low status person in detail). That many do not leave the group can be attributed to the fact that they have few, if any, alternatives which provide them with peer contact. The state of aloneness for those who are driven out seems more unendurable than that of being a low status member of the group. For these reasons the upgrading of low status persons is frequently one of the therapist's goals for the group.

In groups where the status differential is extreme (incongruent), the aversiveness of the group tends to increase, and its very existence is threatened. Exline and Ziller (1959) created various status patterns by means of role instructions to the participants. Their results show that groups having incongruent patterns manifest significantly more conflict and are less stable than those having congruent patterns. Therefore, if the therapist expects to create a group situation which is reinforcing to all members, he may have to reduce the degree of incongruence of status.

Fortunately the status structure of the group is not static. Persons can acquire skills, resources, and even symbols of a higher status member through behavior modification procedures. Empirical support for this assertion is found in a study by Bavelas, Hastorf, Gross, and Kite (1968). The writers demonstrated in four-man laboratory groups that it was possible to raise the status of low status individuals. The procedure used was to reinforce with lights the verbal contributions of low status individuals (a green light flashing at their desk was an indication that they were on the right track) and to extinguish those of higher status individuals. As a consequence, the relative verbal production of the low status persons increased as did their rank on a sociometric test. The implication for the therapist is that differential reinforcement of group members for the performance of highly valued activities alters the relative ranks of members.

In another laboratory study, Burnstein and Zajonc (1965), by manipulating the appearance of success or failure on a simple group task, were able to improve the status of low status members and to lower that of the top status members in four-man groups. They also found that as a person's status improves, his performance level goes up. One implication for the group therapist is that the performance of an individual can be improved if he and his fellow group members are given the notion that he is performing well.

When most of the criteria for a given level of performance are public, the low status client must improve his performance to raise his status. If highly valued activities of the group are already in his repertoire, the therapist may simply reinforce their performance, while withholding reinforcement from the higher status members for the same activity. This approach presents two problems. First, in most children's groups there is a norm about fairness; all resources must be equally shared including the therapist's praise. This norm is especially important in the early phase of group treatment. The second difficulty is that many low status individuals have few skills in their behavioral repertoire which can be reinforced. Under these conditions it may first be necessary to train the client in valued activities which no one else in the group possesses. It is then not necessary to ignore a similar performance by a high status person. At one meeting the activity was a quiz on wild animals. The therapist tutored Wilbur on this subject several weeks before. Since the group valued intellectual accomplishments, they responded by praising Wilbur, who had frequently been called a "retard" at past meetings.

In this example the members themselves reinforced the low status member's performance because it was in an area which they valued. In the following example, the therapist makes it possible for the low status person to use skills he already possesses to earn the group a highly desired reward. Even though the skill is not valued by the group, the reward is. The Tigers valued sports skills more than any other. Henry, who was poorly coordinated, could not compete with the other members in any sport; as a result he was continually abused and teased. The therapist said that the group could go on a fishing trip when they earned enough points, which were to be credited for each hour of studying and each passing grade on the next report card. Henry was the only one in the group who was passing more than half his courses and who studied more than once or twice a week. When totaling the points for the group, the therapist added in Henry's contribution last and carefully pointed out that Henry was the one who pushed the group over the line. Later the therapist also taught Henry some judo so that he could excel in a sport that no one else knew much about in order to maintain his new-found status in the group.

The role instruction procedure can also be used to modify status patterns within the group. The therapist writes several role descriptions and distributes them to members. In these instructions he upgrades the role of a low status person by providing him with information and resources the others do not have. Moreover, he instructs the person to perform behaviors normally performed only by high status members. If the behaviors are not within the repertoire of the low status person, the therapist instructs him prior to the meeting in these behaviors. The status change effected utilizing this procedure is usually temporary; but repeating it on other occasions and using additional procedures such as reinforcement should increase the probability of a stable and generalized shift in the role structure.

Although in some cases the low status person is obvious to all, frequently he is not discovered until he has left the group or has been driven out, and then it is too late to rectify the situation. For this reason, therapists should ascertain as early as possible the relative status of group members. Sociometric tests are an excellent source of data concerning the status of members. The danger in their use is that the therapist may structure his attitudes toward individuals based on insufficient data. To reduce or eliminate a lack of data, they can be obtained in respect to a given task: asking which group member each wants to have on his team, to help him with his homework, to be his monitor for a behavior assignment, to work out a role play or skit is sufficiently nonthreatening and yet is an effective source of additional information.

Leadership Structure

One particular form of high status is that of leadership. If leadership can best be described as a set of behaviors which facilitates group goal attainment or maintenance of the group, then all persons in the group can perform some leadership behaviors. The group usually considers *the* leader to be the person who performs the most highly valued services for the group. However, in most groups more than one person is regarded as leader, and even these choices change from time to time.

In most treatment groups the therapist performs the major leadership behaviors initially. He takes the most relevant steps for maintaining the group, establishing goals, and setting up means by which they can be achieved. However, as the group members have some successes, they begin to imitate his leadership behaviors. Some members naturally emerge as leaders; but the therapist must facilitate the performance of at least some leadership behaviors by all members of the group.

What is the value of members' performing their own leadership behaviors? First, practice in performing leadership functions with respect to treatment goals extends the member's area of competence to other social groups where leadership is usually highly valued. (And, as a result, leadership skills learned in the treatment group are reinforced in other groups.) Second, the more the members provide their own leadership, the more likely that they themselves will work on behaviors which concern them, using methods which are acceptable to them.

For the above reasons the therapist is constantly concerned with training all members in leadership behaviors and transferring his responsibilities to them. In fact, by the end of treatment members should be helping to clarify problems, suggesting treatment plans, developing contracts for each other, choosing their own tasks, and organizing role plays. The therapist shifts roles from leading to prompting. Training in leadership behaviors occurs in the same way as training in all other behaviors which a therapist attempts to increase. He reinforces all approximations of leadership behavior in the group. He points out what he as a model does and sets expectations (group goals) that members should assume some tasks. He uses rehearsal procedures to provide members with practice as leaders of the group. He encourages members to elect one of their number as therapist for a meeting, with himself acting as cotherapist. Some therapists set up leadership seminars for adolescents in the later phases of treatment in order to focus directly on extending their leadership skills. In these seminars, discussion-leading skills are taught as well as skill in discussion participation, and strategies for getting one's ideas across in a group meeting are handled. After treatment has terminated some members may serve as group aides, for which they are trained in an in-service program which further reinforces their leadership ability. (See the end of Chapter Fifteen.)

One of the most effective leadership training procedures is cross-age tutoring (Lippitt, 1969). Children in a treatment group are enlisted to tutor younger children outside the group. The older children have learning or behavioral handicaps of their own which are the major targets of change. As most of these clients have few teaching skills, they tend at first to rely heavily on punishment, of which they themselves have often been the recipients. The treatment group then shifts its focus to teacher-training, and the clients are taught basic skills of tutoring. The therapist trains the tutors through role playing, discussions with the classroom teachers of the tutorees, interviews with younger children about what they expect from tutors and how they like to be treated. Tutoring plans are developed in the group and are evaluated following the tutoring sessions. Thus each member assumes a leadership position outside the group for which he is trained within the group. Such a position is highly valued by most clients, and often the therapist makes them earn the right by requiring certain levels of behavioral change. For those children whom nothing seems to interest, the role of tutor often is the exception. Another advantage is that the client is not forced to remain in the role of the person being helped. As a result his evaluation of himself as "troublemaker" appears to change radically, and his overt behaviors change accordingly.

Lippitt (1969) discusses many variations of cross-age tutoring. One was used by a behaviorally oriented social worker in the following way. Four problem children (ages ten and eleven) in one classroom were chosen as tutors for four younger boys (ages seven and eight) from a special education class. The maladaptive behavior of the older children included fighting, stealing, and out-of-seat behavior. Tutoring occurred in the younger boys' class once a week for twenty minutes for desk work and for twenty minutes in the gymnasium for foursquare and dodge-ball. Prior to each contact with the children the clients met in a group with the social worker to prepare for their tutoring sessions and to evaluate the previous session. Occasionally the classroom teacher was present. For their work with the younger children the boys received a salary in points which could be used for desired trips. Although no data were collected on the classroom behavior of either group, both teachers reported improvement in overall behavior, and the teacher of the older boys indicated that they became enthusiastic about school.

Communication Structure

A common problem in discussion groups is the dominance of one or two people and the withdrawal of others (see Chapter Twelve). To attain individual treatment goals, it is frequently desirable to obtain an even distribution of communication and participation in discussion and other activities.

One way to modify the distribution of communication within the group is to give each member a stopwatch and, if necessary, teach him how to use it. After all members demonstrate competence in the use of the watches, each measures the amount of time the neighbor on his right speaks. At the end of fifteen minutes, the therapist writes down the names and the times on the blackboard as in the first two columns of Table 3. The group then has the task of equalizing the time spoken by dividing the fifteen-minute period among five people. The low participants, however, have to be given some help to participate. A brief discussion follows on what should be talked about, and members are encouraged to take notes. With young children the therapist puts the notes or hints on the board. A brief practice session takes place, and then each member again times the neighbor on his right. Warnings are given when the three-minute limit is reached. If no member goes thirty seconds above

TABLE 3

	Time 1	Ideal	Time 2
Mary	2:30	3	3:25
Therapist	4:10	3	3:00
Alice	0	3	2:35
Louise	7:10	3	2:47
Helen	1:20	3	3:03

or below the allotted amount, the group may be reinforced. If someone exceeds the three-minute limit at least one person has to fall below it. The group then repeats the previously described process and tries again. Regardless of initial success, multiple trials are essential in order to stabilize the new communication pattern. In addition to multiple trials, gradually increasing the time from fifteen minutes to the whole treatment period is an effective device for achieving stabilization. Also, each person begins to time himself after the second or third trial. (The therapist is also clocked. It often comes as a surprise to him that he is either as active or as passive as the statistics imply.)

There are a number of variations on this technique. One is to use counters instead of timers to record the number of times each person thinks another person is rewarding or punishing him. This technique is especially effective in groups where the interaction is primarily of a punishing nature. The definition of reward or punishment is based on the interpretation of each individual. Once a baseline is established, a group goal may be set in which, for example, the total number of rewarding statements must be doubled and punishing statements halved. Later goals may be set to eliminate punishing statements entirely.

Another situation involves the use of subgroup competition. The group is divided into two or more subgroups, and a baseline is established for each subgroup in terms of either the distribution of communication or the reinforcement-punishment ratio (see above). After a total group discussion on a given topic, outcomes are compared. The winning subgroup is the one which most nearly approximates the desired distribution or ratio. Both (all) subgroups may win since each is competing against its own baseline. In another variation only certain content is timed. For example, in one group only problem-oriented talk in which the member blamed no one but himself for his problems was timed. In another group (of depressed adolescents in a mental institution) only positive self-references were counted. Does this approach stabilize the new distribution, ratios, or content? The general impression of therapists who have used it is that it must be employed episodically in order to maintain the desired structure. One or two additional primings seem to be enough to maintain the desired pattern.

The recapitulation technique, in which the participant must summarize what the person before him said, is another useful device for redistributing the degree of participation in a group. It is especially effective in curbing dominating individuals who do not listen to others but use others' talking time to plan their own statements or who do not listen but respond only to cue words. This form of confrontation is less aversive than more direct forms in that most individuals discover for themselves their nonlistening behavior patterns as they attempt in vain to recapitulate their predecessors' remarks. On occasion, the therapist profits most from this procedure.

Normally this procedure has to be applied for only a short period to get the necessary effect. However, to give member practice in listening and monitoring their listening, repeated trials at various intervals are recommended. If continued for too long a period, the conversation can become stilted, non-task oriented, and aversive. The procedure is more effective if used as a novelty or sporadically as the situation calls for it rather than regularly.

Taping the meeting and replaying the tape is also an excellent exercise for confronting members with their dominance in the communication structure. Usually this procedure is followed by the recapitulation or the stopwatch technique mentioned above in order to train group members in the desired new behaviors.

Subgroup Structure

In most groups communication is not distributed equally in direction as well as in quantity. That is, members tend to communicate more frequently with some than with others. They tend to choose to play or work in teams more with some than with others. These mutual preferences for work, play, or communication lead to subgrouping.

Such subgrouping is an inevitable part of any group. In the beginning especially, members have difficulty interacting evenly with everyone else. Only within subgroups do some children make friends, a skill lacking in the repertoire of many clients. As a result therapists usually encourage subgroup activities to get children to participate at all. More often than not the subgroup activity enhances rather than detracts from the attainment of most group goals. However, on occasion the subgroups may be valued by the members so much more than the group as a whole that their relationships tend to disrupt the ongoing group process. At this point the therapist makes demands for some minimal participation in group activities.

For the child who is having difficulty approaching other children, a technique called subgrouping or pairing off is often used as demonstrated in the following example. Jay was referred to the group by his mother, who said he had no friends and he often cried. In the group he seldom talked to anyone except occasionally to Larry, who was also somewhat shy. During the course of the meeting, the therapist put Jay and Larry, who had good throwing arms, together in a team for the sandbag throw. (He chose an activity which was likely to result in some success in order to avoid an aversive outcome.) Later, at clean-up, the therapist asked them both to help him (which for these group members was reinforcing). At the next meeting, he noticed that the two boys were sitting together, so he assigned them each the task of monitoring the other's behavioral assignment to be performed in the classroom that week.

In using this procedure the therapist must be careful to avoid putting together people who tend to punish one another.

There must be some basis for positive interaction. But if the two have exactly the same problem, they can be of little help to each other because their interaction tends to reinforce the problem. The balance is not always as clear as in the example above.

It should be clear from the content of this chapter that modification of group structures also involves and has as its purpose the modification of individual behavior. However, if one attempts to modify the behavior of an individual without regard to the norms of the group, the status of the individual, and the communication pattern in the group, the likelihood of success is slim. Changes in group structures like alterations in the level of attraction must be considered as group goals, which if attained result in stable and desirable changes in the behavior of the participants within the group. In the following chapter I discuss still other methods for transferring the changes once learned in the group to home, playground, and school.

14

As the Group Ends

In the beginning it was a neat group. We had a lot of fun and got tokens and all kinds of things. We played games, made up skits, and didn't get much homework. After a while it got harder and harder to get tokens. We began to spend most of our time looking at the assignments we did and getting ready for the next one. At the end there weren't any tokens or food, or anything, although we did go on a lot of trips. Now I'm in the Boy Scouts; it's sure a lot more fun. It's even fun to play with my brothers now.

Throughout this book I have been concerned with the transfer of behavioral change beyond the boundaries of the treatment situation. If the goal of treatment is effective social behavior, this is attained only when the child functions appropriately in the family, school, playground, and other social situations where he acts and is reacted to during most of his waking hours. It is surprising, given the importance of this transfer, that few writers have given it much consideration. Goldstein and others (1966) and Lang (1965) are two major exceptions. Much of this chapter is derived from their observations and my own applications of their postulates. I have also drawn heavily from Ellis (1965) whose interest is the transfer of academic learning. The principles of transfer listed below are neither exhaustive nor mutually independent, representing as they do an early attempt to order and exemplify them in relation to group treatment: (1) gradually increase the similarity between treatment and extra-treatment situations; (2) vary as many aspects of treatment as is organizationally feasible; (3) increase the degree of unpredictability of the treatment situation; (4) increase the degree of client responsibility; (5) increase extra-group incentive; (6) encourage overlearning of the original subtasks; (7) conceptualize the learning after a variety of specific examples; and (8) prepare the client for an unsympathetic environment.

Simulating the Nontreatment World

Ellis (1965, p. 70) suggests that a "teacher should teach under conditions which are at least somewhat similar to the ultimate testing situation." The ultimate testing situation in behavioral treatment is the home, school, playground, or city streets, most of which the treatment situation should simulate and eventually move toward. As Goldstein (1965) points out, one of the major deterents to most forms of therapy is the sharp distinction between the sterile therapeutic chamber and all extra-therapeutic situations. Even the group therapy room usually has too many specific characteristics to generalize readily to other situations. For this reason, as treatment progresses group meetings take place in store fronts, classrooms, clients' homes, playgrounds, and streetcorners, the therapeutic group is gradually modified to include friends from school and the gang, and the program gradually simulates the activities of the street, school and playground. Similarity with extra-group situations is also augmented through behavioral rehearsals and assignments. Behavioral rehearsal can approximate the threatening situation prior to living in it; assignments push treatment completely out of the therapeutic setting into the everyday world of the client.

In the initial and early-middle phases of treatment the group environment is varied as little as possible in an effort to reduce anxiety and increase cohesiveness. Only variation which keeps the program interesting and goal oriented is introduced. When the attractiveness of the group is high, substantial variation can be tolerated. Nevertheless, most therapists will introduce it gradually with a high degree of preparation for each change, especially in the beginning (this tends to desensitize the more anxious members). As the group members gain experience in dealing with change, revisions occur more unexpectedly and with less advance notice. Since frustration and surprises are common to most social groups, the members must practice dealing with them.

Varying Conditions of Treatment

Research has repeatedly demonstrated that cues regularly correlated with reinforcement eventually gain control over the associated behaviors (Bandura, 1969, p. 616). What is frequently referred to as self-reinforcement may be no more than the presence of these cues minus the reinforcement. Variation, therefore, tends to expand the cues under which the behavior is reinforced and increase the likelihood that a variety of cues, rather than externally administered reinforcement, will control the behavior. It is only then that behavior tends to stabilize and generalize.

A child may learn to control his temper tantrums in a playroom in the presence of a therapist and other children of the same sex, but unless he practices this control in a wide variety of social contexts it is unlikely that the control will transfer to the home, school, or unknown future situations. If the therapist alters the location and other physical conditions of the treatment meeting, two purposes are served: he increases the chances to approximate the client's nontreatment context and he provides more situations in which the client can try out his new behaviors. The more varied the circumstances of training, the greater the likelihood that the client will be able to deal with unforseeable stress: behaviorally rehearse as many different situations related to each problem as the client and group can tolerate; vary the conditions under which behavioral assignments are to be performed; gradually reduce control of monitoring procedures; and vary the locale and personnel involved in treatment.

Similarly the greater the variety of reinforcers in treatment, the more likely these reinforcing stimuli will transfer to social situations outside the group. Tokens are too specific to treatment; since praise and other verbal reinforcement are certainly more common reinforcers in the outside world, these too must be included. Reinforcers commonly found in the classroom, the work situation, the playground, the home, should be utilized in treatment. When these are not already in the client's repertoire, they must be paired with existing reinforcers. As I have already pointed out in Chapter Six, most clients have limited reinforcement repertoires. One of the therapist's tasks is to increase that repertoire so that a wide variety of extra-treatment reinforcement will be effective. If one wishes to increase a behavior's resistance to extinction, an intermittent and irregular reinforcement schedule should be followed. Token reinforcement and praise are given at first for every accomplishment. With time, reinforcement is withheld for longer and more varied intervals until, eventually, the irregularity or infrequency of reinforcement in the outside world is simulated. Regular reinforcement should be maintained for the first eight weeks of treatment. If erratic reinforcement is introduced too soon the client may revert to baseline frequencies of behaviors or terminate.

Because clients must learn to respond appropriately to new stimuli, unpredictable situations are intermittently introduced in the later treatment phase. The previously punctual therapist is ten minutes late. The meeting room is changed suddenly; a surprise guest is introduced. A meeting may be postponed. The therapist leaves ten minutes after the meeting has begun. The group is asked to do physical work on behalf of the agency. Although these are common surprises for community center groups, for the client they may represent stressful situations with which he must learn to cope. As the group demonstrates that it can deal with such situations, both frequency and newness are increased.

Shifting Responsibility to Clients

Another termination principle involves the gradual shifting of responsibility from the therapist to the group members. Although client involvement has always been considered a good thing in group work and much of group therapy literature, the arguments have tended to be more moralistic than pragmatic. I propose that client involvement is a necessary step in the transfer and stabilization of change; if clients initiate and perform the therapeutic tasks themselves they are able to resolve the inevitable crises and problems which will occur following termination. Clients must have the skills, of course, to deal with their own problems or those of their peers. Premature delegation of responsibility results, as some writers have noted, in increased aggression, pairing off, avoidance, and clinging dependency (Bion, 1952).

Although the therapist using a behavioral approach is very active in the first phase of treatment, step by step his part in monitoring behavioral change is reduced as the client begins to assume responsibility. As soon as the client gives any indication that he can plan his own behavioral assignments, he participates in designing not only his own but those of his peers. By the termination or final phase of treatment, the client defines the nature of the problem, designs the treatment approach, and evaluates outcomes himself.

Increasing Outside Incentives

Another principle, suggested by Goldstein and others (1966), is to "increase the size of extra-therapy incentives" as a means of transfering change. In general, as the therapist reduces the rewards of the treatment situation, he should help parents and teachers increase their repertoire of reinforcing behaviors and the frequency with which these behaviors and even material reinforcement occur.

Clients are trained to approach and participate in other

groups such as clubs, Boy Scouts, and the YMCA. Their reinforcing repertoires are built up to include reinforcers characteristically provided by other groups. Parents are trained to be major reinforcing agents. Group therapists reduce the frequency of their reinforcing activity so that the relative incentive value of nontreatment situations increases. Detailed discussion of this principle follows in the section on termination of treatment.

Overlearning

Overlearning—that is, more trials and situations than necessary to gain initial learning—can also facilitate transfer. Early manifestation of a desired behavior is not a guarantee of stabilized learning. When each set of new behaviors is taught in multiple situations and under a variety of conditions, however, learning appears to maintain itself and to transfer to other situations. Behavioral rehearsals involve the performance of repeated responses to many persons. When in doubt, rehearsals and assignments should be repeated until it is quite probable that the behavior will occur whenever appropriate.

Learning the General Category

Lang (1965) suggests the extremely important principle that the therapist should move from reinforcement of the specific adaptive behavior to reinforcement of the more general category to which it belongs. If the impulsive child is initially reinforced for counting to ten before he responds to frustrating situations, he should be reinforced at some stage in treatment for all the varieties of self-control which he displays. Otherwise he learns the adaptive behavior in a specific situation but fails to learn it with regard to types of behaviors for which he has not been reinforced. Although specificity is essential in the initial phases of treatment, one should not remain too long at this phase. It behooves the therapist at some point later in treatment to train the client in the general areas of honesty, self-control, assertiveness—all under a wide variety of stimulus conditions.

Ellis (1965, p. 72) urges the teacher to "make sure that

general principles are understood before expecting much of transfer." Goldstein and others (1965, p. 217) also conclude "that transfer can take place as a result of learning of general principles." This principle can be applied to group treatment: the therapist, after a series of behaviors have been learned, asks the group members to point out the general principle involved in them.

Ellis (1965, p. 72) states that in order to conceptualize learning, a wide variety of concrete examples are required. The group situation lends itself to a variety of behavioral examples by virtue of its plural membership representing multiple problems. Furthermore, the general principle involved in a specific set of new behaviors is frequently made explicit in discussion among the members of the group. (If the client is told the general principle prior to learning a series of concrete behaviors, however, he is apt to view the principle as "moralistic," or aversively didactic, until specific actions and their consequences are clear to him.)

When adolescent groups, in particular, prepare for concretizing their gains, increasing use is made of group and self-evaluation of achievement. These discussions are not unlike sensitivity or encounter sessions except that they are guided by specific themes and members are protected by the therapist and group norms from harassment by other members. Each client can accept or reject his peers' observations and suggestions.

Preparing for Unsympathetic Environment

Most of our clients live in a world which has conditioned their behavioral problems and has a vested interest in maintaining them. Although, in most cases, teachers and parents may be trained to react differently to the client, the client must be in part prepared to deal with an unsympathetic environment. In the first behavioral group I organized, a child who was rewarded for staying home after 10 p.m. was subjected to such pressure by his neighborhood peers that our rewards lost their potency. I later trained him through modeling and behavioral rehearsal to develop arguments for staying at home and it became standard practice to prepare each client for arguments from friends, siblings, well-meaning grandparents, parents, teachers, and others who viewed him as "sick," "delinquent," "a nuisance," and yet continued to reinforce those very behaviors.

The standard procedure is to model a discussion in which the "significant others" try to lead the client astray. The therapist usually plays the client role while the client plays the role of the significant other. This is followed by a rehearsal with the client in his own role. The goal is to train the client in a wide variety of counterarguments. Practice in protherapeutic statements appears to facilitate protherapeutic actions. Procedures for making the environment more sympathetic are discussed in detail in the next chapter. Cooperation of the significant persons in the client's environment following treatment is probably one of the greatest contributions to maintaining and transfering change.

Termination of Treatment

Group relationships frequently develop a high degree of intensity in a short period of time; yet one day these relationships must end. Since many clients have a history of unsuccessful relationships, their abrupt ending may be a highly upsetting experience. Special procedures can facilitate termination of the individual's relation to therapist and fellow group members but the procedure used is dependent on the different types of termination. The first type is the individual termination—the client who either has attained his goals or for any reason has decided that he will no longer attend group meetings. The second type is the group termination. Many group members begin and leave treatment together and quite frequently the treatment period for these groups overlaps with the school year (usually because of convenience rather than therapeutic consideration). The third type is the subgroup termination. Several members terminate for such reasons as: their goals were easier to attain than the others; they were in the group longer; or they have been transferred to another treatment group. In the fourth type the therapist may end his relation to the group but it continues treatment with a new leader.

Although most therapists prepare for termination, it

appears that the preparation is often haphazard or contrived at the last moment. It is my experience that if termination is treated casually much of the gain of treatment can be lost. My own approach is to introduce the fact of termination at the first session. The time limits of the group, should they exist, are mentioned as part of the treatment contract and means of terminating earlier or later than the formal date are also introduced. Periodically, the therapist uses natural opportunities to discuss termination. For example, when the children are beginning to plan for their summer vacation, the therapist may point out that the group will end at that time and encourage the group to discuss the implications. When the therapist is ending his relationship to the group, this should be mentioned as early as possible and the group assured that someone else will take his place.

At least two months before treatment ends, termination becomes a regular item on the meeting agenda. Clients begin to make specific plans; group meetings occur less frequently; phone calls are often substituted for meetings and finally even the calls are faded and termination is completed. When individuals or subgroups terminate, the terminating members are encouraged to share their post-treatment planning with the other members. This usually reinforces the planning activities of the terminating members and provides models for those who remain. During the period in which termination is taking place the retiring members frequently assume leadership positions in the group: they may meet with the therapist to help plan meetings or serve as models for those members who are in an earlier phase of treatment. Occasionally, a terminating subgroup will separate from the larger group to deal with common problems of termination, before finally losing contact with the therapist and the agency. In this case they may meet either with or without the therapist, the latter procedure being more recommendable.

In the Valley View School for Boys, St. Charles, Illinois (see Rose and others, 1971b) a special group has been set up which deals solely with the problems of termination. The boys earn the right to join the group by passing through several other formal statuses, each of which requires a certain degree of behavioral control. The termination group is set up like a seminar for the discussion of such problems as re-entering and staying in school, getting along with parents, obtaining and keeping a job, staying away from highly seductive delinquent peers, and relations with the parole officer. Each member is helped to make his final plan for termination after he has demonstrated his ability to deal with relevant problem areas. Even in correctional institutions, however, some members are so attracted to the group that they will set themselves up to fail so they will not be required to leave it. As is often the case with clients for whom the treatment group has been their first successful group experience, it becomes necessary to increase the attractiveness of alternate groups.

The first step is to help members find friends outside the group. A set of assignments is given toward the end of treatment which consists of successively more difficult approach responses to neighbors, children on the playground, classmates, and acquaintances at work. Clients are encouraged to contact peers with fewer behavioral problems than themselves and as their new relationships progress, they are encouraged to bring their new friends to the meeting. Activities pair the client and his new friend(s). The client is then urged to plan activities in which he spends time usually reserved for group meetings with his new friend(s).

The second step is to decrease the attractiveness of the therapist. Just as the client is trained to approach new friends, he is also trained to approach and interact with new adults or those adults with whom his relationship had previously been uncomfortable. If possible, these adults are also trained to approach the client. They are invited to group meetings and to participate in activities designed to strengthen the new sub-group. In many groups therapists are now experimenting with family interaction therapy in the final phase. The sibling or parent role-plays certain difficult social situations and, with the help of other sets of clients and their families, attempts to find alternate ways of dealing with these situations.

Third, the attractiveness of outside activities is increased.

In the course of treatment the group member is introduced to a number of other organizations, and when he receives at least minimal reinforcement in such a club, he is helped to attend their meetings.

Group meetings in the final phase, then, consist almost solely in reporting the results of new encounters and extra-group activities. The meetings become briefer, less frequent, and more business-like. There is no sentimental last meeting. Although such an experience may be useful when the therapist is attempting to increase the attractiveness of the group, it is incompatible with trying to reduce it.

One facet of termination often overlooked is that no matter how successful treatment has been some behavioral set-backs may occur. Contrary to parole regulations the juvenile offender may be seen in the company of an adjudicated delinquent; an aggressive client may be forced into a fight in which he is caught by the principal; a fearful child may have a bout with nervousness. The therapist should prepare the client for such events; many problems can be avoided if the client is prepared with a specific telephone number to call, a specific person to ask for, or a specific place to go in case problems do arise again. Discussion of a case example in the group may be useful and models who have called for help can also be recruited to discuss with the group the conditions under which they may need help.

Once the group therapist has mastered these procedures, he is ready to initiate group treatment. The importance of these principles can not be underestimated since change in the group has little or no meaning for the child without change beyond the group. In fact, this is the long-range aim of all our change endeavors. But even with mastery of all the principles discussed in this and previous chapters, the group therapist can not do the job alone. He requires the assistance of families, teachers, sometimes the police, group aides, and other treatment staff to complete the job. How these people are involved and trained in treatment is the subject of the next and final chapter.

15

Training for Treatment

When the therapist called Mrs. B about a home assignment, she asked whether the therapist would give her some pointers on how to make life more liveable with Pat at home. The therapist told her about the group and suggested that the three of them, in developing assignments for Pat, work on behavior that was getting him in trouble at home. The therapist also agreed to send Mrs. B a copy of the book Living with Children, *which explains the principles he was using in the group, and to talk again with her about how she could apply these principles.*

Although the therapist may be of considerable help to the client, he is a direct influence for only a few hours a week, at most. What happens to his client in the approximately 105 other waking hours of the week must necessarily concern the therapist. By assigning the child tasks to perform in the school, at home, in the street, and on the playground, the therapist begins to extend treatment into major portions of the week. However, this is often insufficient to overcome familial or school contingencies and attain and maintain treatment goals. Reinforcement of completed assignments at the meeting sometimes occurs too late to be effective; monitoring procedures often break down at home or in school; and in the course of the week problems arise which need to be dealt with immediately.

For these reasons teachers, parents, friends, and other significant persons in the child's everyday environment are encouraged and trained whenever possible to become facilitators of change. They are shown how to use many of the procedures which have been effective in the treatment group. This is no easy task. Gaining access to many of these individuals is in itself difficult. But the results are usually worth the effort. In a review of outcomes of cases of juvenile offenders in the Hartwig Project (Rose and others, 1970), it appeared that when social workers could enlist cooperation of both parents and teachers the children were almost always successful in attaining treatment goals. Where one or the other was cooperative, a majority of the children seemed to improve; and where neither was cooperative, only a few of the children showed and maintained significant gains.

The significant other needs to be trained in either monitoring the child's behavior or application of change procedures or both. He must understand the relevance of what he is to do, and have some understanding of the theory behind it. The plan should hold out some promise of success and there should be some reward for him in cooperating with the therapist. (Of course, the greatest reward to parents and teachers would be the reduction of the child's nuisance behavior.) The therapist should help significant others deal with the practical barriers to monitoring or the use of change procedures. If teachers and parents are totally disinterested, it is usually best to focus one's attention on those significant others who are willing, at least minimally, to cooperate. In the case of the family, there is often a concerned grandparent, uncle, aunt, or older sibling who will help in treatment but, in any case, monitoring must take place primarily in that area where cooperative adults are present. There is the possibility that treatment effects in one area will transfer to the other and that as the child improves in one area adults in the other will become more willing to cooperate.

Working With Teachers

What types of assistance does the group therapist generally ask from teachers? Foremost is help in assessing and monitoring. Often it is the teacher who, in thirty hours per week of contact with the client, has spotted the problem and made the referral for treatment. The therapist should contact the teacher and ask him or her to delineate the problem in more specific terms. It is often necessary to ask the teacher to fill in a checklist or even to count on a time-sample basis the frequency of problem behaviors. (If the original request for outside help was made as a means of getting rid of the child and the problem, the teacher may find herself involved in far more work than she had expected.) Monitoring of a baseline usually does not mean an end of counting; it must be continued in order to ascertain whether changes are occurring. The frequency of monitoring may be reduced to fit the teacher's workload or other time-saving devices may be instituted, but as long as the problem continues, monitoring must also.

The therapist will eventually give the child behavioral assignments to perform in the classroom. Again the teacher is asked to observe and perhaps sign a note saying that the assignment was performed. Frequently the assignments will be determined by the therapist and teacher together; such assignments tend to be more willingly monitored by the teacher than those which come to her as accomplished fact. On occasion the teacher will be asked to institute change procedures. However, this rarely happens without a prior request from the teacher. Teachers frequently express a desire to be helpful in additional ways and when they are acquainted or willing to become acquainted with the fundamentals of behavior modification, their assistance as direct behavior modifiers may also be utilized.

In general, the treatment procedures taught to the

teacher focus on increasing praise, reducing the frequency of criticism, increasing the ignoring of behaviors which, though annoying, do not disturb the group, training in the setting of monitorable rules (limited in number), and keeping the class to those rules. (See Madsen, Becker, and Thomas, 1968, for a more specific account of how these procedures operate.) Teachers who want to go further are taught how a classroom token-economy works, as well as how to utilize natural classroom reinforcers such as the tape recorder, films, free time, and trips. Teachers familiar with these reinforcement procedures may also be helped to master modeling and rehearsal procedures.

Although there is a great deal of literature on the training of teachers as behavior modifiers, most of it is from the standpoint of behaviorists who have finally made major inroads into the given school. Most group therapists, on the other hand, are likely to find themselves the first to have utilized behavior modification in the school. A psychologist, counselor, or social worker who has only recently entered the school situation often has to establish his credibility before he can request the cooperation of teachers in such activities as monitoring, reporting child's progress to the therapist, or creating situations which facilitate the performance of adaptive behaviors. For this reason, it is not always as easy as most of the literature suggests to contact and work with teachers as additional facilitators in the treatment process.

The therapist who has entered a new school and hopes to gain the teacher's cooperation in some aspect of treatment should make a few assumptions. The teacher has only limited time. (Initially the therapist has only five to ten minutes with any teacher.) Most teachers have many classes and very limited time to do their preparation. They may have been imposed on previously by psychologists, counselors, or social workers who asked them to take on additional burdens, often without results. In light of the teacher's understandable hesitancy, the therapist must be prepared for his brief conference with a number of ideas on the specific types of cooperation he is seeking and the help he can offer the teacher in return. It will save time if this is typed and given to the teacher after the initial contact.

If possible, volunteers—parents, older children, or university students—are used to assist the teacher and therapists in monitoring classroom behavior. Of course, some teachers prefer not to have classroom observers. In this case it may be preferable to ask the teacher to do a limited time-sample observation of the behavior or, if that is too difficult, to fill out a checklist. A checklist is the least desirable form of monitoring because due to its generality it is the most susceptible to teacher bias. If broad categories, such as "Did he get out of his seat today?" or "Did he hit another child this afternoon?" are used, bias can be avoided. These types of responses tend to be very reliable if accumulated in short periods each day for several days. (See Suratt, Ulrich, and Hawkins, 1969, for a discussion of the pronounced advantages of using older students as behavioral engineers.)

The teacher needs "rewards" too. The teacher's cooperation is inevitably dependent on what the psychological payoff is for her. If the client is disturbing the class, a reduction of the disturbing behavior would, indeed, be reinforcing to her. As soon as possible after initial contact, it is helpful for the therapist to provide some type of service for the teacher in order to establish himself as a useful person. If he has demonstrated that he can take care of a child who is acting out and disrupting the classroom, the teacher is more likely to talk about other problems and if he makes himself available for consultation about classroom problems in general most teachers will respond positively. Teachers are experts, too. Respect for and utilization of their ideas are necessary to maintain communication and to effect the best possible plan. All too often, the enthusiastic behavior modifier overwhelms the teacher with ideas that she herself long ago conceived of and put into practice. In many cases, too, teachers, especially recent graduates, are familiar with principles of behavior modification but have had little support in applying their ideas. The group therapist may provide that support by getting permission from higher administrative levels to which he may have access and helping design a plan to facilitate classroom treatment by the teacher.

There is some danger in seeking the teacher's cooperation with a child not previously recognized by her as problematic. The child may be identified by the teacher as someone who deserves unusual types of attention and although this is not usually the case, one should consider the possibility before the teacher is approached. This is especially true for children who have a history as juvenile offenders. Knowledge of this may lead the teacher to regard such children as inherently hostile or untrustworthy, for example. The therapist should be wary of involving the teacher who has shown indications that she will be unable to deal with such clients.

Teachers rightfully resent implications of blame. If a teacher is unable to control a child even after several suggestions have been made, the principal or therapist may suggest that it is solely her fault that the technique is not effective or that control cannot be achieved. Considering the fact that most teachers have thirty to forty children, several of whom probably have behavior problems, her lack of success in dealing with one or two can hardly be considered an indication of incompetence.

Working With Parents

After school, in the evenings, on holidays, and on weekends, most children are the responsibility of their parents. Certainly a large part of problematic behavior takes place in the home and parents are frequently the source of referral for treatment. They claim they cannot manage the child, that he is too "sick" for them to handle alone, or that he is so disruptive no one else gets any attention. Many parents want help and are willing to work to assist in the process. Others want help, but because they have failed so often in the past, they are dubious about what they can do. Still others want to send the problem off to the therapist and be done with it.

When parents are highly motivated, the major locus of treatment can very well be the home and the major change agent the parent. The role of the therapist in these cases is primarily training the parents in the procedures they need for dealing with their child's specific problems. The therapy group may be regarded as an auxiliary source of help, a place where the child can try out new peer-related behaviors and experiment with controls learned at home or in the group. When the family, for whatever reason, is unwilling to cooperate, the child's treatment group (or the school) becomes the major locus of therapy and the family is the auxiliary source of assistance.

I will deal primarily with auxiliary involvement of parents and although I refer to "parents," it is often an older sibling, a grandparent, an aunt, or uncle who is most interested. Methods of gaining and maintaining their assistance are the same as for teachers: parents will be requested to spell out the problem in specific detail; they will often be asked to count the manifestations of a behavior or set of behaviors; they will be encouraged to monitor completion of behavioral assignments and to sign the assignment before it is returned to the therapist. At their request they might be taught some of the principles of behavioral learning and will be helped to apply them. In the process of assisting the therapist, a parent often becomes sufficiently interested in the process and its outcome that he requests training for himself and his spouse as behavior modifiers.

When possible parents may be organized into orientation or training groups. The orientation group is designed primarily to disseminate information about the children's groups. One or two sessions are usually sufficient. Case examples and brief descriptions of group meetings are presented and discussed. The focus is on showing parents how to monitor and explaining the behavioral assignment and some of the basic principles. If possible, the meeting can be used to ferret out specific behaviors the parents feel should be changed and some effort is made to get parents to justify their selection of a particular behavior.

In many cases these groups develop into programs for training parents as behavior modifiers of their own children. (See Rose, 1969, and Holland, 1970, for a fuller exposition of program content.) In the training group, parents are taught how to assess their children's problems, formulate realistic goals and subgoals in behavioral terms, monitor, and utilize a set of change procedures. The group trainer uses a wide variety of didactic teaching procedures: programmed texts; presentation of model parents; case examples; videotaped models; behavioral rehearsal; and behavioral assignments.

Since many parents' schedules prohibit group orientation, individual home contacts, office visits, or telephone contacts are highly desirable. These contacts are time consuming but without some communication with the parents, treatment of the child is extremely difficult.

Several excellent programmed booklets are available which can be used to teach the literate parent the basic principles of treatment. The two most commonly used programs have been Smith and Smith's *Child Management* (1965) and Patterson and Gullion's *Living with Children* (1968) (also excellent for teachers). It should be pointed out that these booklets (and others which have appeared more recently) are not panaceas and have little value when read alone without opportunity for discussion. Some parents have complained about the over-specificity of the examples, which many cannot identify with their own problems, and assumptions which they cannot accept at face value. In addition, refer to Brown (1971) for an extensive bibliography of literature in the field.

Working With Police

Teachers and family members are not the only adults with whom children come in contact. When working with early juvenile offenders, for example, the therapist may provide his greatest service by training his client in interaction with the police. It is often possible to work with the police and the client at the same time as with the client. If the client has had several contacts with the police and has been labeled a juvenile offender, it may be possible to gain police cooperation in reducing pressure on the client, especially if they are aware that some type of direct help is being provided to the client. A group of therapists who spent most of their time working with juvenile offenders rode in patrol cars to gain perspective on the policemen's view and simultaneously used this period to orient the police to the role of the therapist (see Rose and others, 1970).

Training Treatment Staff

Therapy can seldom occur with the child alone. His parents, concerned relatives, teacher, or probation officer should be involved in the treatment process. And they can often play an active role in such tasks as monitoring the problem behavior and even dealing with the child in a different way than has been their custom. And what about the therapist? Like the other adults involved, he too requires training. Regardless of his background, he usually will need additional training to lead the behaviorally-oriented group. If he is already trained in behavior modification, he needs additional theoretical training in group leadership.

There are three classifications of group therapists. The professional is usually a psychologist, counselor, social worker, or psychiatrist who has had graduate training and practice in some form of therapy. The paraprofessional usually holds a bachelor's degree and has assisted in some form of psychological or social service. The group aide is often a former member of a group or the parent of a member. Most aides have had less than college and some less than high school education.

Everyone preparing for group leadership must first take a course in behavior therapy either in a university or in an agency in-service training program. This course should be primarily designed to teach the application of principles of learning theory in the modification of human behavior. One of the assignments should be to modify someone's behavior (including one's own) successfully. It is also recommended that the aspiring therapist have a course in small group theory, although, if necessary, this can be taught during the training program. Assuming the above background, the trainee is assigned the role of an observer in a group. He is trained to monitor on-going member behavior and may also be asked by the therapist to monitor certain therapist behaviors as well. When he shows proficiency in the use of a timer and counter to record behavior, he will be assigned to count the behavior of several individuals. After this task is completed successfully, he is also assigned the task of charting the data. After each meeting, the trainee's work is discussed with him, corrections are pointed out, and future assignments are made. If there are several observers across several groups, a group supervising session is used in order to provide the observers with a broader range of experiences. (I have used as many as five observers behind a one-way screen. The only requisite is that each have a specific task.)

After he is proficient as an observer, he will be asked to make home and school visits in order to collect extra-group data which he also charts and appends to intra-group data. At this phase he will be involved with the therapist in evaluating the data and revising treatment plans, and given an assignment as a co-therapist. He is now assigned a circumscribed task such as organizing a role-play around a specific problem or leading a group discussion. At the end of the meeting the therapist will point out what he could have done differently and will reinforce him for what he did well. After he has shown initial skill in leading discussions, reinforcing members, dealing with dominant or aggressive individuals, and utilizing limits, he and the therapist trade roles. The supervisory meetings following treatment continue, but even in these the trainee assumes growing responsibility.

After the group has terminated, the trainee becomes therapist for a new group. He is assisted in group composition by the supervisor who gradually fades out in the course of the first few meetings. From here on his work is supervised only by frequent inspection of the data and an occasional visit by the supervisor. This on-the-job training often is run parallel to an in-service seminar in which various problems occurring in the group are discussed. The seminar serves to broaden his experience as well as to provide him with additional supervision.

This model provides the clients as well as the beginning therapist with a great deal of protection. Moreover, there is considerable opportunity to observe good practice from a model. By learning to apply the skills gradually the student tends to become a more disciplined therapist with a greater concern for important details of observation and monitoring.

Training Group Aides

In recent years, increasing use has been made of older high school students or working adolescents as aides in the treatment group. This has been especially valuable in groups which are ethnically or racially different from the therapist. The aide provides a communication link, enhances acceptance of the therapist's message, and is a more effective model for imitation. Aides can also be invaluable help with the vast amount of work that must be performed in a behavioral treatment group: rewards must be distributed, behavior must be observed and sometimes tabulated, role-plays must be organized, behavioral assignments must be checked, and so on. Many therapists find this more than they can handle alone. Multiple leadership facilitates the transfer of learning to the community because it affords several models for the clients. Modeling effects are further increased if at least one of the therapists shares some characteristics with the individuals with whom the client has daily contact (Goldstein, Heller, and Sechrest, 1966, p. 226). For this reason the aide often is only somewhat older than the group members, from the same community, of a similar racial or ethnic background, and a high status person in their eyes. These aides are paid a salary, have staff status, are trained in much the same way as the therapist. However, since most do not have any theoretical training, an in-service seminar provides theoretical formulation in behavior modification and small group theory. There is considerable evidence that aides can be trained in short periods of time (see, for example, Laws, Brown, Epstein, and Hocking, 1971).

The aide also serves as the agency's external link to the community (see Sarri and Vinter, 1967). Rather than being a passive recipient of services, the community is involved by providing through its own manpower a service for itself. This not only makes the service more palatable, it provides jobs formerly assigned only to middle-class outsiders.

Of course, the aides' presence in the clinic or agency does not automatically bridge the vast social chasm between some agencies and the communities they serve. It is frequently, however, a significant step in that direction.

Now that the aides have been trained, the families and teachers have been prepared to assist in the endeavor, and the principles are at the therapist's finger tips, he should be ready to begin. If the aim of this book has been achieved, the reader should now have at his disposal a set of prescriptions for fulfilling his role as group therapist. I do not assume that I have resolved all the issues. But as further experience accrues in the application of behavioral principles to small groups, more of these questions will be answered, and prescription for therapist activities will be extended and elaborated.

Bibliography

ALDEN, S. E., PETTIGREW, L. E., and SKIBA, E. A. "The Effect of Individual-Contingent Group Reinforcement on Popularity." *Child Development,* 1970, *41,* 1191–1196.

AUSUBEL, D. P. *The Psychology of Meaningful Verbal Learning.* New York: Grune and Stratton, 1963.

AYLLON, T., and AZRIN N. *The Token Economy: A Motivational System for Therapy and Rehabilitation.* New York: Appleton-Century-Crofts, 1968a.

AYLLON, T., and AZRIN, N. "Reinforcer Sampling: A Technique for Increasing the Behavior of Mental Patients." *Journal of Applied Behavior Analysis,* 1968b, *1,* 13–20.

BACK, K. "The Exertion of influence Through Social Communication." *Journal of Abnormal and Social Psychology,* 1951, *46,* 9–23.

BANDURA, A. "Influence of Models' Reinforcement Contingencies on the Acquisition of Imitative Responses." *Journal of Personality and Social Psychology,* 1965, *1,* 589–595.

BANDURA, A. *Principles of Behavior Modification.* New York: Holt, Rinehart and Winston, 1969.

BANDURA, A., and WALTERS, R. H. *Social Learning and Personality.* New York: Holt, Rinehart, and Winston, 1963.

BARRISH, H. H., SAUNDERS, M., and WOLF, M. M. "Good Behavior Game: Effects of Individual Contingencies for Group Consequences on Disruptive Behavior in a Classroom." *Journal of Applied Behavior Analysis,* 1969, *2,* 119–124.

BAVELAS, A., HASTORF, A., GROSS, A., and KITE, R. "Experiments on the Alteration of Group Structure." In D. Cartwright and A. Zander (Eds.), *Group Dynamics: Research and Theory.* New York: Harper and Row, 1968, 527–537.

BION, W. R. "Group Dynamics: A Review." *International Journal of Psychoanalysis,* 1952, *33,* 235–247.

BLACKHAN, G. J., and SILBERMAN, A. *Modification of Child Behavior.* Belmont, Calif.: Wadsworth, 1971.

BREGER, L., and MC GAUGH, J. L. "Critique and Reformulation of 'Learning Theory' Approaches to Psychotherapy and Neurosis." *Psychological Bulletin,* 1965, *63,* 338–358.

BROWN, D. G. *Behavior Modification in Child and School Mental Health: An Annotated Bibliography of Applications with Parents and Teachers.* Washington, D.C.: National Institute of Mental Health, 1971.

BUEHLER, R. E., PATTERSON, G. R., and FURNISS, J. M. "The Reinforcement of Behavior in Institutional Settings." *Behaviour Research and Therapy,* 1966, *4,* 157–167.

BURNSTEIN, E., and ZAJONC, R. B. "The Effect of Group Success on the Reduction of Status Incongruence in Task-Oriented Groups." *Sociometry,* 1965, *28,* 249–362.

BUSHNELL, D., JR., WROBEL, P. A., and MICHAELIS, M. L. "Applying 'Group' Contingencies to the Classroom Study Behavior of Preschool Children." *Journal of Applied Behavior Analysis,* 1968, *1,* 55–61.

CARTWRIGHT, D. "The Nature of Group Cohesiveness." In D. Cartwright and A. Zander (Eds.), *Group Dynamics: Research and Theory.* New York: Harper and Row, 1968, 91–109.

CARTWRIGHT, D., and ZANDER, A. (Eds.) *Group Dynamics: Research and Theory.* New York: Harper and Row, 1968.

CARLSON, S. C., ARNOLD C. R., BECKER, W. C., and MADSDEN, C. H. "The Elimination of Tantrum Behavior of a Child in an Elementary Classroom." *Behaviour Research and Therapy,* 1968, *6,* 117–119.

CAUTELA, J. R. "A Behavior Approach to Pervasive Anxiety." *Behaviour Research and Therapy,* 1966, *4,* 99–109.

CHURCHILL, S. "Social Group Work: A Diagnostic Tool in Child Guidance." *American Journal of Orthopsychiatry,* 1965, *35,* 581–588.

CLEMENT, P., FAZZONE, R., and GOLDSTEIN, B. "Tangible Reinforcers and Child Group Therapy." *Journal of American Academy of Child Psychiatry,* 1970, *9,* 409–427.

CLEMENT, P., and MILNE, P. "Group Play Therapy and Tangible Reinforcers Used to Modify the Behavior of 8-Year-Old Boys." *Behaviour Research and Therapy,* 1967, *5,* 301–312.

COHEN, H. L., FILIPCZAK, J. A., and BIS, J. S. *Case I: An Initial Study of Contingencies Applicable to Special Education.* Silver Spring, Maryland: Educational Facility Press, Institute for Behavioral Research, 1967.

COHEN, R. "The Effects of Group Interaction and Progressive Hierarchy Presentation on Desensitization of Test Anxiety." *Behaviour Research and Therapy,* 1969, *7,* 15–26.

COHEN, R., and DEAN, S. J. "Group Desensitization of Test Anxiety." *Proceedings, 76th Annual Convention, American Psychological Association,* 1968, 615–616.

CREER, T. L., and MIKLICH, D. R. "The Application of a Self-Modeling Procedure to Modify Inappropriate Behavior: A Preliminary Report." *Behaviour Research and Therapy,* 1970, *8,* 91–92.

DALEY, M. F. "The 'Reinforcement Menu': Finding Effective Reinforcers." In J. D. Krumboltz and C. E. Thoresen (Eds.), *Behavioral Counseling: Cases and Techniques.* New York: Holt, Rinehart, and Winston, 1969, 42–45.

DAVISON, G. C. "Self-control Through 'Imaginal Aversive Contingency' and 'One-downsmanship': Enabling the Powerless to Accommodate Unreasonableness." In J. D. Krumboltz and C. E. Thoresen (Eds.), *Behavioral Counseling: Cases and Techniques.* New York: Holt, Rinehart, and Winston, 1969, 319–327.

ELLIS, H. *The Transfer of Learning.* New York: MacMillan, 1965.

EXLINE, R., and ZILLER, R. C. "Status Congruency and Interpersonal Conflict in Decision-Making Groups." *Human Relations,* 1959, *12,* 147–161.

FAIRWEATHER, G. W. (Ed.) *Social Psychology in Treating Mental Illness: An Experimental Approach.* New York: Wiley, 1964.

FELDMAN, R. A. "Group Integration, Intense Interpersonal Dislike, and Social Group Work Intervention." *Social Work,* 1969, *14* (3), 30–39.

FERSTER, C. B., and SKINNER, B. F. *Schedules of Reinforcement.* New York: Appleton-Century-Crofts, 1957.

FESTINGER, L. "A Theory of Social Comparison Processes." *Human Relations,* 1954, *7,* 117–140.

FRANKS, C. M. (Ed.) *Behavior Therapy: Appraisal and Status.* New York: McGraw-Hill, 1969.

GINOTT, H. G. *Group Psychotherapy with Children: The Theory and Practice of Play Therapy.* New York: McGraw-Hill, 1961.

GINOTT, H. G. "Group Therapy with Children." In G. Gazda (Ed.),

Basic Approaches to Group Psychotherapy and Group Counseling. Springfield, Ill.: C. C Thomas, 1968.

GITTELMAN, M. "Behavior Rehearsal as a Technique in Child Treatment." *Journal of Child Psychology and Psychiatry*, 1965, *6*, 251–255.

GOLDSTEIN, A., HELLER, K., and SECHREST L. *Psychotherapy and the Psychology of Behavior Change*. New York: Wiley, 1966.

GRAZIANO, A. M., and KEAN, J. E. "Programmed Relaxation and Reciprocal Inhibition with Psychotic Children." *Proceedings, 75th Annual Convention of the American Psychological Association*, 1967, *32*, 253–254.

GUMP, P. V., and SUTTON-SMITH, B. "Activity-Setting and Social Interaction: A Field Study." *American Journal of Orthopsychiatry*, 1955, *25*, 755–760.

HAMBLIN, R. L., BUCKHOLDT, D., FERRITOR, D. E., KOZLOF, M. A., and BLACKWELL, L. J. *The Humanization Processes*. New York: Wiley, 1971.

HANSEN, J., NILAND, T., and ZANDI, L. "Model Reinforcement in Group Counseling with Elementary School Children." *Personnel and Guidance Journal*, 1969, *47*, 741–744.

HASTORF, A. "The 'Reinforcement' of Individual Actions in a Group Situation." in L. Krasner and L. Ullmann (Eds.), *Research in Behavior Modification*. Holt, Rinehart, and Winston, 1965.

HAWKINS, H. L. "Imitative Learning in Therapy Groups Comprised of Chronic Schizophrenic Patients." Unpublished M. A. thesis, University of Oregon, March 1964.

HINDS, W., and ROEHLKE, H. "A Learning Theory Approach to Group Counseling with Elementary School Children." *Journal of Counseling Psychology*, 1970, *17* (3), 49–55.

HOEHN-SARIC, R., FRANK, J., IMBER, S., NASH, E., STONE, A., and BATTLE, C. "Systematic Preparation of Patients for Psychotherapy. 1: Effects on Therapy Behavior and Outcome." *Journal of Psychiatric Research*, 1964, *2*, 267–281.

HOLDER, C. "Temper Tantrum Extinction: A Limited Attempt at Behavior Modification." *British Quarterly Journal of Social Work*, 1969, *4*, 8–11.

HOLLAND, C. J. "An Interview Guide for Behavioral Counseling with Parents." *Behavior Therapy*, 1970, *1*, 70–79.

HOLLANDER, E. "Competence and Conformity in the Acceptance of Influence." *Journal of Abnormal and Social Psychology*, 1960, *61*, 365–370.

HOMANS, G. C. *Social Behavior: Its Elementary Forms.* New York: Harcourt Brace Jovanovich, 1961.

HOMME, L. E., and TOSTI, D. T. "Contingency Management and Motivation." *Journal of the National Society for Programmed Instruction,* 1965, *4,* 14–16.

IHLI, K. L., and GARLINGTON, W. K. "A Comparison of Groups Versus Individual Desensitization of Test Anxiety." *Behaviour Research and Therapy,* 1969, *7* (2), 207–210.

JACOBSON, E. *Progressive Relaxation.* Chicago: University of Chicago Press, 1938.

JULIAN, J. W., BISHOP, D. W., and FIEDLER, F. E. "Quasi-Therapeutic Effects of Intergroup Competition." *Journal of Personality and Social Psychology,* 1966, *3,* 321–327.

KANFER, F. H. "Issues and Ethics in Behavior Manipulation." *Psychological Reports,* 1965, *16,* 187–196.

KANFER, F. H., and PHILLIPS, J. S. *Learning Foundations of Behavior Therapy.* New York: Wiley, 1970.

KATAHN, M., STRENGER, S., and CHERRY, N. "Group Counseling and Behavior Therapy with Test-Anxious College Students." *Journal of Consulting Psychology,* 1966, *30,* 544–549.

KELLAM, A. M. "Shoplifting Treated by Aversion to a Film." *Behaviour Research and Therapy,* 1969, *7,* 125–127.

KELLY, G. A. *The Psychology of Personal Constructs.* New York: Norton, 1955.

KOLVIN, I. "Aversive Imagery Treatment in Adolescents." *Behaviour Research and Therapy,* 1967, *5,* 245–248.

KONDAS, O. "Reduction of Examination Anxiety and Stage Fright by Group Desensitization and Relaxation." *Behaviour Research and Therapy,* 1967, *5,* 275–282.

KRUMBOLTZ, J. D., and THORESEN, C. E. (Eds.) *Behavioral Counseling: Cases and Techniques.* New York: Holt, Rinehart, and Winston, 1969.

LANG, P. J. "The Transfer of Treatment." *Journal of Consulting Psychology,* 1966, *5,* 375–378.

LAWS, D. R., BROWN, R. A., EPSTEIN, J., and HOCKING, N. "Reduction of Inappropriate Social Behavior in Disturbed Children by an Untrained Paraprofessional Therapist." *Behavior Therapy,* 1971, *2,* 519–533.

LAZARUS, A. "Behaviour Rehearsal Vs. Nondirective Therapy Vs. Advice in Effecting Behaviour Change." *Behaviour Research and Therapy,* 1966, *4* (3), 209–212.

LAZARUS, A. "Group Therapy of Phobic Disorders by Systematic Desensitization." *Journal of Abnormal and Social Psychology,* 1961, *63,* 504–510.

LAZARUS, A. A., and ABRAMOVITZ, A. "The Use of Emotive Imagery in the Treatment of Children's Phobias." *Journal of Mental Science,* 1962, *108,* 191–195.

LINDSLEY, O. R. *Training Teachers to Change Environment.* Presentation at the University of Oregon Colloquia on Behavior Modification, School of Education, Eugene, May 1966.

LINDSLEY, O. R. "A Reliable Wrist Counter for Recording Behavior Rates." *Journal of Applied Behavior Analysis,* 1968, *1,* 77.

LIPPITT, P. "Children Can Teach Other Children." *Instructor,* 1969, *78,* 41–99.

LIPPITT, R., POLANSKY, N., REDL, F., and ROSEN, S. "The Dynamics of Power." *Human Relations,* 1952, *5,* 37–64.

LOMONT, J. F., and EDWARDS, J. E. "The Role of Relaxation in Systematic Desensitization." *Behaviour Research Therapy,* 1967, *5,* 11–25.

LOTT, A. J., and LOTT, B. E. "Group Cohesiveness as Interpersonal Attraction: A Review of Relationships with Antecedent and Consequent Variables." *Psychological Bulletin,* 1965, *64,* 259–309.

LOVITT, T. C., GUPPY, T. E., and BLATTNER, J. E. "The Use of Free Time Contingency with Fourth Graders to Increase Spelling Accuracy." *Behaviour Research Therapy,* 1969, *7,* 151–156.

MADSEN, C. H., BECKER, W. C., and THOMAS, D. R. "Rules, Praise, and Ignoring: Elements of Elementary Classroom Control." *Journal of Applied Behavior Analysis,* 1968, *1,* 139–150.

MAHONEY, M. J. "A Residential Program in Behavior Modification." Paper presented at the fifth annual meeting of the Association for the Advancement of Behavior Therapy, Washington, D. C., 1971.

MC FALL, R. M., and MARSTON, A. R. "An Experimental Investigation of Behavior Rehearsal in Assertive Training." *Journal of Abnormal Psychology,* 1970, *76,* 295–303.

MC MANUS, M. "Group Desensitization of Test Anxiety." *Behaviour Research and Therapy,* 1971, *9,* 51–56.

MEYER, J., STROWIG, W., and HOSFORD, R. "Behavioral-Reinforcement Counseling with Rural High School Youth." *Journal of Consulting Psychology,* 1970, *2,* 127–132.

MOWRER, O. H. "The Behavior Therapies, with Special Reference to Modeling and Imitation." *American Journal of Psychotherapy,* 1966, *20,* 439, 461.

MYERS, A. E. "Team Competition, Success, and Adjustment of Group Members." *Journal of Abnormal and Social Psychology,* 1962, *65,* 325–332.

OAKES, W. F. "Reinforcement of Bales' Categories in Group Discussion." *Psychological Reports,* 1962, *11,* 427–435.

PATTERSON, G. R., and ANDERSON, D. "Peers as Social Reinforcers." *Child Development,* 1964, *35,* 951–960.

PATTERSON, G. R., and GULLION, M. E. *Living with Children: New Methods for Parents and Teachers.* Champaign, Illinois: Research Press, 1968.

PATTERSON, G. R., RAY, R. F., and SHAW, B. A. "Direct Intervention in Families of Deviant Children." *Oregon Research Institute Research Bulletin,* 1968, *8* (9).

PATTERSON, G. R., SHAW, D. A., and EBNER, M. J. "Teachers, Peers, and Parents as Agents of Change in the Classroom." In F. A. M. Benson (Ed.), *Modifying Deviant Social Behaviors in Various Classroom Settings.* Eugene, Ore.: University of Oregon, 1969, *1,* 13–47.

PATTERSON, G. R., and WHITE, G. D. "It's a Small World: The Application of 'Time-out from Reinforcement.'" *Oregon Psychological Association Newsletter,* 1969, *15,* 2.

PAUL, G. L. "Outcome of Systematic Desensitization." I: "Background Procedures, and Uncontrolled Reports of Individual Treatment" and "Outcome of Systematic Desensitization." II: "Controlled Investigations of Individual Treatment, Technique Variations, and Current Status." III: "Behavior Modification Research: Design and Tactics." In C. M. Franks (Ed.), *Behavior Therapy: Appraisal and Status.* New York: McGraw-Hill, 1969.

PAUL, G. L., and SHANNON, D. T. "Treatment of Anxiety Through Systematic Desensitization in Therapy Groups." *Journal of Abnormal Psychology,* 1966, *71,* 124–135.

PHILLIPS, E. L. "Achievement Place: Token Reinforcement Procedures in a Home Style Rehabilitation Setting for 'Pre-delinquent' Boys." *Journal of Applied Behavior Analysis,* 1968, *1,* 213–223.

PREMACK, D. "Toward Empirical Behavior Laws. 1: Positive Reinforcement." *Psychological Review,* 1959, *66,* 219–233.

RAVEN, B. H., and RIETSMA, J. "The Effect of Varied Clarity of Group Goal and Group Path upon the Individual and His Relation to his Group." *Human Relations,* 1957, *10,* 29–44.

ROBINSON, C., and SUINN, R. "Group Desensitization of a Phobia in Massed Sessions." *Behaviour Research and Therapy,* 1969, *7,* 319–321.

ROSE, S. D. *Relaxation Procedures for Use in Systematic Desensitization.* Ann Arbor: University of Michigan, 1966.

ROSE, S. D. "A Behavioral Approach to Group Treatment of Children." In E. J. Thomas (Ed.), *The Socio-Behavioral Approach and Applications to Social Work.* New York: Council on Social Work Education, 1967.

ROSE, S. D. "A Behavioral Approach to the Group Treatment of Parents." *Social Work,* 1969, *14,* 21–29.

ROSE, S. D., FLANAGAN, J. F., and BRIERTON, D. *Counseling in a Correctional Institution: A Social Learning Approach.* Paper presented at the National Conference on Social Welfare, Dallas, Texas, May 21, 1971a.

ROSE, S. D., FLANAGAN, J., and BRIERTON, D. *A Behavioral Technology in a Correctional Environment—The Valley View Approach.* Paper presented at the fifth annual meeting of the Association for Advancement of Behavior Therapy, Washington, D. C., September 5, 1971b.

ROSE, S. D., COLES, C., FLANIGAN, B., SHERMAN, J., and FLANAGAN, J. *Behavioral Treatment of Smokers and Weight Watchers in Groups.* Madison, Wisconsin: University of Wisconsin, 1970.

ROSE, S. D., SUNDEL, M., DELANGE, J., CORWIN, L., and PALUMBO, A. "The Hartwig Project: A Behavioral Approach to the Treatment of Juvenile Offenders." In R. Ulrich, T. Stachnic, and S. Mabry (Eds.), *Control of Human Behavior, Vol. II: From Cure to Prevention.* Glenview, Illinois: Scott, Foresman, 1970.

ROTTER, G. B. *Social Learning and Clinical Psychology.* New York: Prentice-Hall, 1954.

SAILOR, W. S., GUESS, D., RUTHERFORD, G., and BAER, D. M. "Control of Tantrum Behavior by Operant Techniques During Experimental Verbal Training." *Journal of Applied Behavior Analysis,* 1968, *1,* 237–243.

SARASON, I. G., and GANZER, V. J. "Developing Appropriate Social Behaviors of Juvenile Delinquents." In J. D. Krumboltz and C. E. Thoresen (Eds.), *Behavioral Counseling: Cases and*

Techniques. New York: Holt, Rinehart, and Winston, 1969, 178–193.

SARRI, R. C., and VINTER, R. D. "Organizational Requisites for a Socio-Behavioral Technology." In E. J. Thomas (Ed.), *The Socio-Behavioral Approach and Applications to Social Work,* 1967.

SCHMIDT, G. W., and ULRICH, R. E. "Effects of Group Contingent Events upon Classroom Noise." *Journal of Applied Behavior Analysis,* 1969, *2,* 171–179.

SCHWARTZ, A. N., and HAWKINS, H. L. "Patient Models and Affect Statements in Group Therapy." *Proceedings of the 73rd Annual Convention of the American Psychological Association.* Washington, D. C.: American Psychological Association, 1965, 265–266.

SCHWITZGEBEL, R. L. "Short-term Operant Conditioning of Adolescent Offenders on Socially Relevant Variables." *Journal of Abnormal Psychology,* 1967, *72,* 134–142.

SCHWITZGEBEL, R., and KOLB, D. A. "Inducing Behavior Changes in Adolescent Delinquents." *Behaviour Research and Therapy,* 1964, *1,* 297–304.

SLAVSON, S. R. "Group Psychotherapies." In J. L. McCarey (Ed.), *Six Approaches to Psychotherapy.* New York: Dryden Press, 1955, 129–178.

SKINNER, B. F. *Science and Human Behavior.* New York: Macmillan, 1953.

SHERIF, M., and SHERIF, C. *Groups in Harmony and Tension.* New York: Harper and Row, 1953.

SMITH, J. M., and SMITH, D. E. *Child Management: A Program for Parents and Teachers.* Ann Arbor, Michigan: Ann Arbor Publishers, 1966.

STAATS, A., and STAATS, C. *Complex Human Behavior.* New York: Holt, Rinehart, and Winston, 1963.

STAMPFL, T. G. "Implosive Therapy: The Theory, The Subhuman Analogue, The Strategy, and the Technique. Part I: The Theory." In S. G. Armitage (Ed.), *Behavior Modification Techniques in the Treatment of Emotional Disorders.* Battle Creek, Michigan: VA Publication, 1967.

STUART, R. B. "Behavioral Control of Overeating." *Behaviour Research and Therapy,* 1967, *5,* 357–365.

STUART, R. B. "Operant-Interpersonal Treatment of Marital Discord." *Journal of Consulting and Clinical Psychology,* 1969, *33,* 657–682.

STURM, I. E. "The Behavioristic Aspect of Psychodrama." *Group Psychotherapy,* 1965, *18,* 50–64.

SUINN, R. M. "The Desensitization of Test-Anxiety by Group and Individual Treatment." *Behaviour Research and Therapy,* 1968, *6,* 385–387.

SURATT, P. R., ULRICH, R. E., and HAWKINS, R. P. "An Elementary Student as a Behavioral Engineer." *Journal of Applied Behavior Analysis,* 1969, *2,* 85–92.

THARP, R. C., and WETZEL, R. J. *Behavior Modification in the Natural Environment.* New York: Academic Press, 1969.

THIBAUT, J. W., and KELLEY, H. H. *The Social Psychology of Groups.* New York: Wiley, 1959.

THOMAS, E. J. "The Socio-Behavioral Approach: Illustrations and Analysis." In E. J. Thomas (Ed.), *The Socio-Behavioral Approach and Applications to Social Work.* New York: Council on Social Work Education, 1967.

TYLER, V. O., and BROWN, G. D. "The Use of Swift, Brief Isolation as a Group Control Device for Institutionalized Delinquents." *Behaviour Research and Therapy,* 1967, *5,* 1–9.

TRUAX, C. B., CARKHUFF, R. R., and KODMAN, F., JR. "Relationship Between Therapist-Offered Conditions and Patient Change in Group Psychotherapy." *Journal of Clinical Psychology,* 1965, *21,* 327–329.

ULLMANN, L. P., and KRASNER, L. (Eds.) *Case Studies in Behavior Modification.* New York: Holt, Rinehart, and Winston, 1965.

ULRICH, R., STACHNIK, T., and MABRY, J. (Eds.) *Control of Human Behavior, Vol. II: From Cure to Prevention.* Glenview, Illinois: Scott, Foresman, 1970.

UNDERWOOD, B. J., and SCHULZ, R. W. *Meaningfulness and Verbal Learning.* New York: Lippincott, 1960.

VINTER, R. D. "The Essential Components of Social Group Work Practice." In R. D. Vinter (Ed.), *Group Work Practice,* 1967a, 8–38.

VINTER, R. D. "Program Activities: An Analysis of Their Effects on Participant Behavior." In R. D. Vinter (Ed.), *Group Work Practice,* 1967b, 95–109.

VINTER, R. D., SARRI, R. C., VORWALLER, D. J., and SCHAFER, W. E. *Pupil Behavior Inventory—A Manual for Administration and Scoring.* Ann Arbor, Michigan: Campus Publishers, 1966.

WAGNER, M. K. "Reinforcement of the Expression of Anger Through Role-Playing." *Behaviour Research and Therapy,* 1968, *6,* 91–95.

WAHLER, R. G. "Peers as Classroom Teachers." Paper presented at the 94th annual meeting of the American Association of Mental Deficiency, Washington, D. C., May 1970.

WEINER, H. "Some Effects of Response Costs upon Operant Behavior." *Journal of the Experimental Analysis of Behavior,* 1962, *5,* 201–208.

WIGGINS, J., DILL, F., and SCHWARTZ, R. "On 'status liability.'" In D. Cartwright and A. Zander (Eds.), *Group Dynamics: Research and Theory.* New York: Harper and Row, 1968.

WILLIAMS, C. D. "The Elimination of Tantrum Behavior." *Journal of Abnormal Social Psychology,* 1959, *59,* 269.

WODARSKI, J. D., HAMBLIN, R. L., BUCKHOLDT, D. R., and FERRITOR, D. E. *The Effects of Different Reinforcement Contingencies on Cooperative Behaviors Exhibited.* Paper presented at the fifth annual meeting of the Association for the Advancement of Behavior Therapy, Washington, D. C., September 1971.

WOLPE, J. *Psychotherapy by Reciprocal Inhibition.* Stanford: Stanford University Press, 1958.

WOLPE, J. *The Practice of Behavior Therapy.* New York: Pergamon Press, 1969.

WOLPE, J., and LANGE, P. J. "A Fear Survey Schedule for Use in Behavior Therapy." *Behaviour Research and Therapy,* 1964, *2,* 27–30.

WOLPE, J., and LAZARUS, A. A. *Behavior Therapy Techniques: A Guide to the Treatment of Neuroses.* New York: Pergamon Press, 1966.

WORCHEL, P. "Catharsis and the Relief of Hostility." *Journal of Abnormal and Social Psychology,* 1957, *55,* 238–243.

ZANDER, A. "Group Aspirations." In D. Cartwright and A. Zander (Eds.), *Group Dynamics: Research and Theory.* New York: Harper and Row, 1968.

Index

D

E

F

G